The Confederate Housewife

The
Confederate
Housewife

RECEIPTS & REMEDIES,
TOGETHER WITH SUNDRY SUGGESTIONS
FOR GARDEN, FARM & PLANTATION

COMPILED AND EDITED
BY JOHN HAMMOND MOORE

SUMMERHOUSE PRESS
COLUMBIA, SOUTH CAROLINA

Published by Summerhouse Press
in Columbia, South Carolina

Summerhouse Press
P.O. Box 1492
Columbia, SC 29202
(803) 779-0870
(803) 929-1175 fax

Manufactured on acid-free paper by
Wentworth Printing Company, Inc., West Columbia, SC

Cataloging-in-Publication Data
The Confederate housewife : receipts & remedies, together with sundry
suggestions for garden, Farm & plantation / compiled and edited by
John Hammond Moore.
      p.   cm.
Includes bibliographical references and index.
ISBN 1-887714-09-X (pbk. : alk. paper)
1. Recipes--Confederate States of America. 2. Cookery,, American-
-Southern style--History--19th century. 3. Home economics-
-Civil War, 1861-1865-Social aspects. I. Moore, John Hammond.
TX153.C58   1997
641.5975--dc21   97-3226
                                                         CIP

DﾹﾹID YOU EVER THINK, BOYS, THERE WAS SO MUCH VIM, AND HOPE, AND ZEAL, AND ENERGY, AND ABILITY IN THE WOMEN OF THE SOUTH AS THE TIMES HAVE SHOWN UP? BLESS THEIR GOOD AND BRAVE AND WARM-BEATING HEARTS, THEY ARE (AND OF RIGHT OUGHT TO BE) THE PRIDE OF CREATION, AND MAN IS BUT THE—WELL, COMPARISONS ARE ODIOUS AND IT ISN'T WORTH WHILE TO RUN OUT THE ANTITHESIS JUST NOW. SOME FOLKS DO SAY THAT OUR "SUBLIME WOMEN" ARE BEGINNING TO FIND OUT THEIR LEVEL IS SEVERAL STRATA ABOVE THAT OF THEIR ASSOCIATES IN THE GENUS HOMO, AND THAT TROUBLES IN THE WIGWAM MAY SUCCEED THESE UGLY DAYS OF STRIFE AND DANGER. NOT A WORD OF IT—NOT A WORD OF IT—DON'T BELIEVE A SYLLABLE OF IT. AND YET THERE ARE SOME FUNNY THINGS TURNING UP NOW AND THEN.

—*Edgefield Advertiser,* February 18, 1863

THE CONFEDERATE HOUSEWIFE

Contents

Acknowledgements

I would like to thank several Columbia residents who have taken special interest in the development of this project and provided much-needed assistance—Sharmila Bhatia, Thelma Hayes, Mel Jenkins, Bill Schmidt, and John and Carolyn Winberry. Food historian Karen Hess of New York City made very helpful suggestions concerning an early draft of the manuscript. Material is quoted, with permission, from Robert Hurley Mackintosh, Jr., ed., *"Dear Martha . . ." The Confederate War Letters of a South Carolina Soldier, Alexander Faulkner Fewell* (Columbia, 1976); papers of Jennie Akehurst and Warren Akin, Special Collections, University of Georgia; David Golightly Harris Journals, Winthrop University Archives; Vanderhorst Papers, South Carolina Historical Society; and at the South Caroliniana Library, University of South Carolina, the diaries of Mary Boykin Chesnut and Emma Holmes and papers of the Mackenzie, McLeod, and McLure families.

Author's Warning!

And a word to the wise. Although every effort has been made to present these recipes, remedies, and household-farm hints as published, one should exercise a degree of caution for at least two reasons. 1.) Directions often are expressed in casual, imprecise terms such as a handful of this or that, add ingredients "to suit your taste," and so on. 2.) Printers sometimes made mistakes, which, when dealing with food or one's health, could prove unfortunate. . . to say the least. For example, the "Remedy for Diptheria" (104) appeared in both *Field and Fireside* and Sumter's *Tri-Weekly Watchman* in October 1862, but hopelessly garbled because of slight (but important) spelling errors such as alder/elder and dogwood/logwood. The recipe for preserving dead bodies (119) experienced similar problems, readers sometimes being advised to keep the "shoulders" (not the shrouding) wet with the prescribed mixture. So forewarned, step into the turbulent world of your great-grandparents—the Confederate States of America.

8

Introduction

Avolume much like this one was conceived in the midst of war thirteen decades ago. Ironically, however, an attempt to combat shortages was itself done in by shortages, specifically a lack of ink, paper, cloth, and perhaps time. Only one "receipt" book was printed within the Confederacy, a slim, twenty-eight-page pamphlet with wallpaper covers produced in Richmond, Virginia, in 1863 by West and Johnston. Since 1960, at least four publishers have reissued this intriguing little curio—*The Confederate Receipt Book: A Compilation of Over One Hundred Receipts, Adapted to the Times.* In addition, the *South Carolina Historical Magazine* recently unveiled another fifty "receipts" apparently assembled in the 1860s.[1] Yet the origins of the latter are somewhat vague, and both collections are far too minuscule to tell us much about homefront life. This volume, inspired by a chance encounter, provides for the first time a comprehensive, grassroots picture of the difficulties many Confederate housewives faced during these tumultuous years. Half of nearly six hundred entries—all published or transcribed during the Civil War—relate to the preparation and cooking of food and encompass both substitutes and standard fare, everything from snow corn cakes and cracker pie to walnut catsup and secession rice bread. These mouth-watering delights are supplemented by random quotations from contemporary sources.

Some thirty years ago, while I was teaching at Winthrop College in Rock Hill, South Carolina, the city librarian, Nan Weller Carson, showed me another scrapbook of Civil War "receipts," or recipes. As I recall, it had belonged to an ancestor of her husband, Paul—perhaps a grandmother, a great-aunt, or some distant cousin several generations back. I do know the lady was a resident of upland South Carolina or Georgia and had contributed recipes to *Southern Field and Fireside,* a periodical published in Augusta, Georgia, during the war. And her handiwork—clippings from that magazine and various country weeklies—clearly was intended for publication as a cookbook.[2] This woman of mystery crossed out some recipes, wrote "mine" on others, and starred several with the words "for book."

Nan urged me to edit this material for publication. In the 1960s, however, the United States was awash in Civil War re-enactments and commemorative galas on a grand scale; by comparison a bunch of old clippings seemed

9

inconsequential, even trivial. In succeeding years she often tried to steer me toward the scrapbook once more: "It wouldn't take long to type up and write a little introduction. You can do it. I know you can." But each time I sought quick refuge in some excuse. Then, about ten years ago, she fell ill, the first step in a steady decline that included long months in several nursing homes. I visited her occasionally and, so long as she could talk, that scrapbook always made its way into our conversations. Once she threatened, while smiling broadly and puffing on a cigarette, to leave "the damned thing" to me. "I'll shame you into finishing it up in a proper fashion," she said triumphantly. "That is just what I'll do."

Nan Carson died in May 1990 at the age of eighty-five, and a few weeks later I was notified that I was among those mentioned in her will. In due time I became owner of a dozen pewter goblets, a heavy crystal owl, a couple of wooden figures, two plaster heads—one a Renaissance lady (I think), the other an Indian chief—and a startling mola from the San Blas Islands near Panama . . . but no scrapbook. Subsequent inquiries produced no clues to its whereabouts, so the collection of Civil War clippings apparently has disappeared.

Yet these artifacts and personal belongings ultimately had what I am sure was the effect intended. The wood carvings and the Italian woman set me to thinking about Nan's request once more, as did the mola, which depicts some sort of wild Central American god who seems about to bring the wrath of ages down upon my fickle, unrepentant soul. To say this multicolored shaman disturbed my sleep would be an exaggeration, but he was on my mind for several months.

At length, a few hours spent with microfilm at the South Caroliniana Library convinced me that, even though the scrapbook had vanished, one could reconstruct much of its contents from the "Housewife's Manual," a column that appeared every few weeks in *Southern Field and Fireside*. Also, contemporary South Carolina and Georgia publications provide still more "receipts" and household hints that Carson ancestors could have collected during the Civil War. These include newspapers printed in various communities within a hundred miles or so of Augusta and, in addition to *Southern Field and Fireside*, another Augusta journal, *Southern Cultivator*, which was issued somewhat erratically in the early 1860s—monthly, semi-monthly, weekly, and often not at all.

Still more gems can be found in *Farmer and Planter*, a Columbia, South Carolina, monthly that ceased operations late in 1861; a handful of little almanacs; and a truly impressive compendium covering some six hundred pages—Francis Peyre Porcher's *Resources of the Southern Fields and Forests*.[3] This massive work, published in Richmond and Charleston in 1863, is a wide-ranging treatise crammed with useful information. Interestingly, Porcher quoted freely

JOHN HAMMOND MOORE

from newspapers, and they, in turn, reprinted his words. On some occasions, local editors cited sources outside of the South Carolina–Georgia area, from cities such as Mobile, New Orleans, Raleigh, and Richmond—communities in virtually every corner of the Confederacy.

In addition, Henry Fulmer of the South Caroliniana Library was able to produce an intriguing, handwritten journal kept by the Alexander McLeod family from 1845 to 1864 in Marlboro District, now Marlboro County, in the eastern part of South Carolina. Like most such volumes, it is a mishmash of kitchen "receipts," poems, knitting instructions, and medical lore (McLeod was a physician); but, in this instance, many items are dated and some obviously were copied from wartime newspapers and magazines. It is, in fact, similar to the Carson collection, although the McLeods transcribed their treasures instead of cutting them out and pasting them in a book.

What follows, then, is only an approximation of Nan Carson's lost volume. All of the material—except perhaps for occasional bits contributed by the McLeods—was published in inland South Carolina and Georgia, a sprawling expanse within the Confederate States of America that remained largely untouched by actual warfare until the fall of 1864. This region was, for nearly three years, insulated from enemy incursions and generally united in its devotion to "The Cause"—at least it was not, like New Orleans, subject to the heel of "Beast" Butler, nor did residents from the outset openly oppose Jeff Davis, as some did in Virginia, Tennessee, and Alabama. Probably no other part of the Confederacy could have produced a collection such as this. Some area newspapers continued to publish, albeit in much reduced form, and an occasional journal also staggered along as best it could, resulting in an on-the-spot portrait of day-to-day life in wartime found nowhere else.

Taken as a whole, this advice on cooking, cleaning, household chores, and farming sheds considerable light upon the homefront. Naturally enough, substitutes for scarce items such as coffee, soap, candles, flour, and leather loom large, as do schemes for preservation of foodstuffs. Since ice was one of the war's first casualties, the threat of spoilage concerned many housewives, although it would be wrong to assume that the poor and those living in rural areas relied heavily upon this northern monopoly.

Nearly all of these wartime "receipts" are short, sometimes almost too much so, and proceed at once to get down to business. Virtually every household seems to have had its own formula for making vinegar and fashioning hard and soft soap from materials at hand. Directions for brewing beer are plentiful, and ways to concoct puddings abound. The latter emphasis may result from ease of preparation and the fact that cooks, in this manner, could use up odds and ends without recourse to precious flour and yeast. Nevertheless, puddings—a fixture in the English diet—were popular in southern homes in peacetime, too. An Alston family cookbook at the South Carolinana Library, a volume compiled in the early nineteenth century, describes a dozen kinds of puddings, everything from ratafia, marmalade, transparent, and plum (usually spelled "plumb") to mixtures of coconut and millet. And the meteorological observations of James Kershaw of Camden, also at the South Caroliniana Library, include directions for making still more puddings—flour, bread, bread and butter, baked rice, apple, orange, custard, steak, marrow, and Yorkshire.

Putting food on the table was, of course, only part of the Confederate housewife's busy routine. In addition to being cook and gardener, she also had to deal with sickness, disease, and household pests and perhaps take on farm and plantation chores normally performed by father, husband, or son. As a result, one finds in these pages advice on how to measure land, estimate the amount of hay in a stack and corn in a crib, stain wood, make shoes from squirrel skins, drive a team of oxen, and collect opium for use in the home. Since a good wife had to be prepared for almost any emergency, there are "cures" for everything from onion breath, warts, colds, and aching teeth to snake bites, piles, diphtheria, hog cholera, dog mange, and cancer. She also is told how to break young steers to the yoke, erect fence posts, tell the age of a horse, and recover precious salt from the floor of her smokehouse.

Omissions from these snippets of household and agricultural lore have relevance, too. Little time is wasted on soups and on cooking meat and poultry because few needed guidance of that sort. Preparation of vegetables for the table and garden salads are treated in the same cavalier fashion—after all, almost anyone can boil collards, slice cucumbers, and shred lettuce without step-by-step instructions. Somewhat puzzling, nevertheless, is the absence of the words "cookies" and "barbecue" and the limited concern shown for tea. Of these three, cookies are the easiest to explain. They existed but traveled under other names such as wafers, macaroons, jumbles, or "little" cakes. One suspects that, as shortages increased, some "big" cakes of those hectic years were not much more than large, flat cookies.

The Carolina Housewife, originally published in 1847 and reissued several times since then (most recently by the University of South Carolina Press in 1979 with an introduction by Anna Wells Rutledge), describes over eighty kinds of "tea cakes" and "tea breads," but says little about the beverage itself and is silent concerning barbecue. During the war years, only a handful of substitutes for tea were offered to Confederate faithful, while almost every adult southerner concocted some bizarre form of ersatz coffee. The list is long, long indeed, and includes, among other things, parched okra seeds, rye, yams,

JOHN HAMMOND MOORE

The Death of Our Old and True Friend Rio!

[In January 1862 the colonel of the Palmetto Riflemen, a group of Anderson County volunteers then in winter camp near Centreville, Virginia, announced that coffee rations would cease. A few days later the men held a parade and mock funeral as they buried a coffeepot. A lengthy, heartfelt eulogy ended with these words.]

Therefore upon the grave of our departed one, let us clasp to our bosoms our only remaining and *spiritual* friend "Bourbon Rye." In conclusion we will sing the following lines:

Oh! come my friends and comrades brave,
Come stand around poor Coffee's grave!
With humble thought and quiet tread,
To place in cold and lonely bed,
Our poor friend Coffee, who is dead.
The loss is great, Oh! let us sigh,
For Whisky now is very high;
It is indeed my honest dread,
That *all our drinks* have forever fled,
For poor friend Coffee now is dead.
We beg the "officers" please to try,
If nothing stronger, give us Rye;
For one and all, our wives have said,
That they would *break* you, like a thread,
If any of us should be dead.
And now kind friends we'll bid adieu,
To Coffee, Rye, and Whisky, too.
And if our Government nought but Molasses can give,
We promise, like Marion, upon Potatoes to live.
                                 —*Charleston Daily Courier*, January 20, 1862

corn flour, corn kernels, cotton seed, ground-nuts (peanuts), and seeds produced by benne and milk-vetch plants and persimmon trees.

Several factors help to explain this mad scramble. Between 1790 and 1860 American consumption of coffee grew from four million pounds per year to over two hundred million, while tea imports rose only from three million to thirty-two million pounds per year.[4] In the 1840s, for example, it was not un-usual for the Charleston market to auction off two or three thousand bags of Rio coffee in a single week.

Not surprisingly, this upsurge of popularity created a demand for cheap coffee long before 1860. In December 1789, the Philadelphia publication *Columbian Magazine* lauded a German physician who had invented "acorn" coffee, to be taken straight or mixed with the real thing. Ten years later, Swedes were drinking "coffee" made from the flour of rye and yellow potatoes. And between 1800 and 1825 other American journals praised "roasted potato" coffee (2/3 potatoes, 1/3 coffee) and brew made from grape seeds, yellow wa-ter flag, and chicory.[5]

Although Germans spearheaded this search for substitutes, the chicory version (often called "Germanic" or "Westphalian" coffee) made the greatest inroads in France and is still available in some form today, notably in New Orleans. Americans fighting in Mexico in the 1840s discovered coffee made from local beans, and at about the same time South Carolinians could buy "Essence of Coffee" in their markets.[6] Tea, on the other hand, obviously was less popular; but, of greater significance, raspberry leaves, various native herbs, and sassafras (leaves, bark, or roots) provided a reasonable wartime substi-tute. As a result, tea was taxed ten percent under tariffs levied in June 1861; coffee was exempt from all import duties.

The barbecue story is much more complex. A pioneer cookbook, *The Virginia House-Wife,* first published in 1824, tells readers how "to barbecue shote." This turns out to be, however, one-fourth of a young hog baked in an oven with a bunch of seasonings. The recommended condiments are garlic, pepper, and salt mixed with red wine, mushroom catsup, and water. Author Mary Randolph says the gravy can be thickened with butter and flour, and those who wish may add sugar.[7]

The more familiar outdoor barbecue of today certainly was known in most parts of the South by that time. Charleston merchant William Richardson attended one held near Camden during a race meet staged in March 1773. Various writers described similar gatherings in the decades that followed.[8] Most seem to have been mass feedings held to celebrate a holiday, lure voters to a political rally, or—in the 1830s and 1840s—to promote railroad construc-tion. As such, they were of little concern to housewives. Slaves did the cook-ing; and, as with sliced cucumbers and garden salads, there was little reason to record a recipe, if indeed any existed. The entire process probably was viewed as an essentially male and somewhat primitive exercise unworthy of female attention.

JOHN HAMMOND MOORE

It is quite possible that—at least to mid-century—these occasions were little more than alfresco animal roasts, without the tomato, ketchup, mustard, and pepper-vinegar concoctions now associated with a good plate of barbecue. But our war with Mexico (1846–1848) wrought great change, for men who returned brought with them a passion for hot peppers as well as the seeds to grow them. In the decade that followed, the use of peppers and vinegar increased dramatically. This gourmet shift is reflected in newspaper ads and cookbooks of that era and in occasional personal correspondence as well.[9] Sweet barbecue quickly passed into oblivion, and animal juices, brimming with flavor, no longer fell sizzling onto coals beneath but were used to baste the meat, much as had been done indoors for generations.

On the eve of the Civil War, we are told, Scarlett O'Hara nibbled on dainty beaten biscuits and partook of barbecue at a grand gathering held at "Twelve Oaks". Perhaps. But most of the wartime barbecues held in South Carolina and Georgia appear to have been all-male affairs.[10] Two years after fighting ceased, a basic recipe for barbecue sauce finally appeared in print—entry no. 260 in Mrs. A. P. Hill's *Housekeeping Made Easy*—"butter, mustard, red and black pepper, vinegar." Most regional cookbooks published during the next half century or so contain at least a rudimentary scheme for making barbecue sauce. Mrs. S. R. Dull's *Southern Cooking* (Atlanta, 1928), however, was among the first to devote several pages to barbecue and tell readers how to dig a pit and go about the business of roasting rabbit, pork, beef, and lamb.

In that same decade, the Roaring Twenties, the commercial South was awakening to the charms of this sectional (even national) treasure. By 1930, Andy's Barbecue had opened in the 2200 block of Atlanta's famed Peachtree Street, and soon residents of Savannah, Charleston, Columbia, Charlotte, and other communities were feasting on barbecue sandwiches that usually cost fifteen cents, only slightly more than the standard ten-cent hamburger. Since that time no southern city, regardless of how small, has been without its neon signs for "Barbecue," "Barbeque," "Bar-B-Cue," "Bar-B-Q," or "B-B-Q." Take your pick.

The challenges that coffee substitutes and barbecue pose for any gastronomic Sherlock Holmes are minuscule compared to the overriding question of where editors found the "receipts" and assorted suggestions they published during the Civil War years. Nineteenth-century journalists reproduced the work of rivals without a shrug, often without acknowledging any debt to those individuals. In fact, information of this sort was copied so casually and so frequently that one is hard-pressed to point to origins and perhaps should not even make the attempt. As food historian Karen Hess observes in her introduction to *Martha Washington's Booke of Cookery* (New York, 1981), American

THE CONFEDERATE HOUSEWIFE

cooking is rich and varied, "a tapestry of extraordinarily complex design." This holds true even when one tries to probe a mere four years of our past. Some entries that follow, for example, clearly reflect the strains of war; others do not and first appeared in peacetime.

A dozen or so items found in the *Confederate Receipt Book* (Richmond, 1863)—among them directions for making spruce beer and cheap blacking, preventing skippers in ham, and curing bacon, camp itch, and croup—appeared earlier in newspapers published in Spartanburg, Edgefield, and Atlanta. But the trail hardly ends there. Suggestions printed in the 1860s for making suet candles, toughening earthenware, and preventing gapes in chickens (utilizing virtually the same words in each instance) were previously set forth in the columns of Pendleton's *Farmer and Planter* (1850–1851). And two decades before that, Charleston's *Southern Agriculturalist* offered up grape seeds as "coffee," told housewives how to make rice griddle cakes (copied from the *New England Farmer*) and loaf rice bread (courtesy of the *New York Farmer*), and advised—in phrases reprinted thirty years later—how to cure "sick" headache and treat wounds in cattle. The "Chinese Method of Mending China," included in this volume, has even more age on it. A strikingly similar paragraph can be found among meteorological data recorded in 1799 by James Kershaw of Camden.[11]

One bit of Civil War advice that clearly was published originally, or nearly so, in the pages of the *Southern Agriculturalist* of July 1838 is a list of rules for the conduct of an overseer. Ostensibly composed by a Colleton District planter a few weeks earlier, these dictums somehow found their way into the *Southern Recorder* of Milledgeville, Georgia, in May 1863 and thus are included in this volume. Even an occasional paragraph that sounds as if it were inspired by desperate times can be misleading. A recipe for "peach leaf yeast cakes" (not identical to the one reproduced in this volume) appeared in the *Southern Agriculturalist* of July 1854.

But saying that one editor copied from another who copied from yet another merely takes us around in circles. One truth that can be stated is this: these wartime "receipts" did not come from traditional cookbooks such as those honoring "housewives" of Virginia, South Carolina, and Kentucky. They came instead, at least in the first instance, from agricultural publications, almanacs, and works such as the second edition of Phineas Thornton's *Southern Gardener and Receipt Book.*[12] Thirty-two of his cooking and household suggestions, often word for word, appear in these pages—everything from green corn pudding to doughnuts, "rye" coffee, mending china with oyster shells, and restoring tainted meat.

Upon reflection, it is obvious that almanacs, farm journals, and how-to-

JOHN HAMMOND MOORE

do-it books are the sort of materials one would expect to find in a nineteenth-century newspaper office; and, when a printer needed to fill out a column of type, he might find in them a few lines that would do the job and perhaps titillate readers. Interestingly, a well-thumbed copy of the 1845 edition of Thornton now in the South Caroliniana Library bears the signature of Charles Calvo, Jr., a man associated with Columbia area newspapers in the late nineteenth century.

Yet another truth should be apparent: an original recipe or a truly innovative household or farming hint is a rare thing indeed. But such items do not have to be entirely new to be of interest. Instead, they only have to offer promise of immediate or potential benefit, and therein lies the contemporary appeal of these wartime "receipts" and suggestions. Perhaps only a handful of readers gave much thought to coffee substitutes in 1860; a year later their ranks were increasing rapidly. In much the same manner, ways to preserve food, make soap, and care for animals (especially if menfolk were in uniform) took on new significance. Put another way, these bits of advice for kitchen, garden, and plantation tend to reveal pressure points in Confederate society. Not every editor catered to such concerns, but some did, especially those turning out agricultural monthlies such as *Southern Field and Fireside.*

Many of these snippets of wartime lore lived on after 1865; however, their genealogy is confounded by several subsequent developments. With peace, cookbooks such as that of Mrs. A. P. Hill no longer stressed simplicity, nor were they circumscribed by shortages. Thus the basics still might be there but so lavishly attired as to be well nigh unrecognizable. In the 1860s, for example, the McLeods of eastern South Carolina—adhering to the good words of Phineas Thornton—used four dozen ears of corn, a pint of milk, and half a pound of sugar to make green corn pudding. Three decades later, the mixture for only six ears required a quart of milk, six eggs, a teaspoon of lemon essence, a cup of sugar, and an unspecified amount of butter.[13]

Another change was editorial: the decision circa 1900 to list whatever is required, not express such matters in paragraph form. Nevertheless similarities persist. The directions found here for making ham toast are expressed in much the same manner in the *Spartanburg Dames' Recipe Book* (1902). Ingredients and suggested amounts are the same and several phrases printed by the *Farmer and Planter* in June 1861 are repeated.

Both puzzling and intriguing is a pickle that meanders through the second half of the nineteenth century with a strange, mixed-up name. In 1847, Sarah Rutledge told readers of her *Carolina Housewife* how "To Make Atzjar," spelled "Atsjar" in the index, although she corrected this error in 1851 and, for good measure, added "Atzjar—No. 2." Among new material inserted in the 1860 edition of Thornton's *Southern Gardener and Receipt Book* is "Adds Jar Pickle."

17

The following year, South Carolina's *Due-West Telescope* published the "receipt" for "Axe Jar Pickles" found in this volume, and in 1895 Atlanta Exposition ladies offered up directions for making "Ax-Jar Pickles."[14]

The ingredients are strikingly similar in each instance, although the Atlanta matrons suggest tossing a pint of rum into a mixture of vinegar, nutmeg, mace, ginger, allspice, cloves, mustard, garlic, and other spices. After 1900 this heady brew, with or without rum, seems to have become the basis for what were known as "universal" or "mixed jar" pickles. As Karen Hess notes in *The Carolina Rice Kitchen* (Columbia, 1992), the word first used to describe this delicacy actually comes from the Persian term *achar*—usually spelled *achaar* in India—and was known in South Carolina as early as 1700. Since Rutledge led off her pickle parade with "Atzjar," an all-inclusive scheme for pickling almost anything, I first thought the original recipe might have been for "A to Z" pickles, but this turned out to be merely an uninformed guess. In any case, the word, not being well understood, was easily transformed through the years into Adds, Axe, Ax, and so on.

Despite confusion such as this and changes such as the lavish use of eggs, butter, and milk in peacetime, it is obvious that these Civil War "receipts," remedies, and household-farming hints have relevance. They repeated, perpetuated, and passed on bits of information that found their way into hundreds of southern households, not just that of Nan Carson's relatives, and thus became in varied form an integral part of our cultural heritage.

One can approach the pages that follow on different levels. For some, they are a window to a bygone era, while minds of more practical bent will discover basic, bare-bones recipes that can be "improved" with a bit of this or that. The McLeod family's soup mix is, after all, merely another version of crock-pot cookery, and the Virginia Stew can be enhanced with the addition of celery and various herbs.

Moving away from the dinner table, still other readers will be amused by various remedies and cures and intrigued by the care of horses and schemes for estimating the weight of live animals. The war years were, in fact, a cultural filter for southern life. In a time of stress and shortage, unusual conditions on the homefront created circumstances that re-ordered everyday priorities. Although difficult to prove conclusively, it appears that the well-to-do suddenly found themselves eating and living much as their less affluent neighbors had been doing for decades. This meant recourse to substitutes and handmade goods that—to the masses—were neither unique nor innovative. They had long been drinking cheap coffee, wearing homespun, preserving food without ice, and making do with less.

In a very general way, the most pressing shortage in the urban South was food, not processed or manufactured goods; in rural areas, the reverse was

JOHN HAMMOND MOORE

true. If one lived in Charleston, Columbia, Savannah, or Atlanta, such things as clothing, luxury items, even spices, sugar, and coffee—though costly—were available throughout the entire war, thanks largely to blockade runners. Those residing in smaller communities or in the countryside enjoyed a more varied diet but had limited access to many commodities once found on the shelves of local stores.

Except for momentary disruptions caused by enemy incursions and the depredations of deserters and renegade cavalry during the last months of the struggle, few went hungry during the war. South Carolina was, after all, an agricultural state with only two real cities; and, as residents fled from Charleston after mid-1863 to escape Federal shells, food actually became more plentiful there. Conditions in Georgia were somewhat different. It could boast of more urban centers and encompassed much more territory. Savannah, the major port, was sealed by Union action in April 1862 (but not captured until December 1864), and Georgia felt the wrath of Sherman first. Nevertheless, as in South Carolina, many towns and villages never heard a shot fired in anger. The truly bad times, actual starvation, came after the war, not during. In fact, farmers had only one good harvest (in 1868) between 1865 and 1870. Ben Robertson had it right when he wrote in *Red Hills and Cotton* (71), "My grandparents never forgot Lee's surrender and the days of starvation in the South."

Since there is little to be gained by reproducing obvious printer errors, punctuation and spelling in the items that follow have been standardized somewhat. Many, as already indicated, come from *Southern Field and Fireside*, the only publication to maintain, with some degree of consistency, a column for Confederate housewives. If two or more consecutive items are from the same issue of a newspaper or appear together in a journal or book, the source is cited at the *end* of the excerpt.

To preserve the original flavor, these fragments of the Civil War era are presented in the same general format utilized by West and Johnston when they produced the *Confederate Receipt Book* in 1863. Those gentleman boasted their "Over One Hundred Receipts" were "Adapted to the Times." One can say the same of this volume.

Notes
1. See Frances M. Burroughs, "The Confederate Receipt Book: A Study of Food Substitution in the American Civil War," *South Carolina Historical Magazine* (January 1992), 31–50. None of the "receipts" cited in this article are reproduced in the pages that follow.

THE CONFEDERATE HOUSEWIFE

2. Daily papers published in larger communities such as Charleston, Columbia, Savannah, Macon, and Atlanta, perhaps because they had telegraph connections and more news to report, as well as more advertising, printed fewer "receipts" than weeklies.

3. The full title is *Resources of the Southern Fields and Forests, Medical, Economical, and Agricultural. Being also a Medical Botany of the Confederate States; with Practical Information of the Trees, Plants, and Shrubs.*

4. William Lerner, chief director, *Historical Statistics of the United States: Colonial Times to 1970* (Washington, 1975), 2:902.

5. *Monthly Magazine and American Review* (September 1800), 238; *Lancaster (Pa.) Hive* (June 12, 1805); *Christian Observer* (April 1804), 245; *Analectic Magazine* (January 1818), 82; and *American Farmer* (March 28, 1825). On June 26, 1861, Mrs. James L. Petigru remarked in a letter to her grandson "that in the War of 1812 I remember well Rye coffee, was used, mixed with the other" (Vanderhorst Papers, South Carolina Historical Society).

6. The *Charleston Daily Courier* (November 20, 1851) said for only 12 1/2 cents a housewife could "save 4 lbs. of store coffee."

7. Karen Hess, ed., *The Virginia House-Wife* (Columbia, 1984), 63.

8. Emma B. Richardson, ed., "The Letters of William Richardson, 1765–1784," *South Carolina Historical Magazine* (January 1946), 6–7. See, for example, Friedrich Gerstacher's description of an Arkansas barbecue held in 1843, translated by Ralph Walker and published in *Early American Life* (August 1984), 30–31, 75; "My Uncle Simon's Plantation" in the *Southern Literary Gazette* (October 21, 1848); and "Good Eatings" in the *Southern Literary Messenger* (May 1863), 304–11.

9. Compare issues of the *Charleston Courier* published in 1845 and 1855 and the 1847, 1851, and 1855 editions of *The Carolina Housewife*. See also the Sarah Hicks Williams Papers, File #3210, Southern Manuscripts Collection, University of North Carolina at Chapel Hill. In addition, various contemporary journals such as the *Southern Cultivator* (February 1850) and the *Southern Christian Advocate* (February 8, 1850) reflect keen interest in peppers.

10. In the late 1930s, several popular magazines (see *Collier's*, September 4, 1937) credited *Gone with the Wind* with creating widespread interest in barbecue grills and barbecued food. However, this trend appears to have originated in California somewhat earlier, avidly promoted by local architects and articles in publications such as *Country Life, American Home, Better Homes and Gardens,* and *House and Garden.* For examples of actual southern gatherings, see the descriptions in the *Edgefield Advertiser* (August 7, 1861), Columbia's *Daily South Carolinian* (April 23, 1864), and the *Albany Patriot* (September 22, 1864).

11. Eight volumes of Kershaw diaries at the South Caroliniana Library cover the years from 1791 to 1825. The volume for 1797–1800 contains about seventy household hints and "receipts." Some of the latter are attributed to established sources such as eighteenth century cookbooks published by Hannah Glasse and E[liza?] Smith.

12. This book by a Camden horticulturist first appeared in 1840 and was reprinted five years later in Newark, New Jersey. Interestingly, a subsequent 1860 edition (produced in Philadelphia) contains Mary Randolph's "barbecued shoat" recipe and over twice as many pages on pickles, vinegar, and catsup sauce.

13. Mrs. Henry Lumpkin, compiler, *Tested Recipe Cook Book* (Atlanta, 1895), 30. This volume was reissued in 1984 by the University of Georgia Press as *The Atlanta Exposition Cookbook,* edited by Darlene R. Roth.

14. Ibid., 28–29.

JOHN HAMMOND MOORE

The Confederate Housewife

Coffee, Tea
& Assorted Potables

WAR COFFEE. A very good coffee can be made, costing only 12 1/2 cents, by mixing one spoonful of coffee with one spoonful of toasted corn meal. Boil well and clear in the usual way. I have used it for two weeks, and several friends visiting my house say they could not discover anything peculiar in the taste of my coffee, but pronounced it very good. Try it, and see if we can't get along comfortably even while our ports are blockaded by the would-be king.—*Tri-Weekly Watchman,* July 8, 1861

ACORN COFFEE. This is one of the best substitutes for coffee, and is much used in Germany. The acorns are shelled, split, dried, and roasted like coffee. When taken out of the roaster, a little piece of butter is put on them. It may be used alone or with real coffee.—*Farmer and Planter,* January 1861

COFFEE! COFFEE! COFFEE! In these days of blockades, when coffee is scarce, prices high, and in many places none to be had at any price, many substitutes are to be tried. I am glad to have it in my power to recommend a substitute which is so nearly like the genuine article as to satisfy the most delicate taste and deceive the oldest coffee drinkers. It is as follows: Take the common *Red Garden Beet,* pulled fresh from the ground, wash clean, cut into small squares the size of a coffee grain or a little larger, toast till thoroughly parched, but not burned, transfer to the mill and grind. The mill should be clean. Put from one pint to one and half, to a gallon of water, and settle with an egg as in common coffee. Make and bring to the table hot—with nice, fresh cream (not milk) and sugar. I will defy you or anybody else to tell the difference between it and the best Java.—*Laurensville Herald,* September 20, 1861

A GOOD SUBSTITUTE FOR COFFEE. Take some brown sugar, says the *New Orleans Picayune,* and burn it perfect black. Then add hot water till it is reduced to the consistency of syrup, and put it in a bottle ready for use. For six persons, take five tablespoonfuls of the liquid and put it in your coffee pot; then put in the dripper one tablespoonful of ground coffee, and drip the boiling water through the syrup, in such a quantity as suits your taste. It is now ready for the table, where it is prepared in the usual manner with milk and sugar. To the above proportions can be added more coffee, if you have it to spare. The burnt syrup will keep any length of time. Care must be taken not to pour the burnt syrup through the dripper.—*Southern Federal Union,* May 13, 1862

CORN & RICE COFFEE. Parched rice also has been used as one of the substitutes for coffee. A correspondent of the *Mobile Register* (1862) says that corn and rice mixed in equal parts, ground, and boiled, make an excellent substitute. As the grain of corn is harder than that of rice, it needs more browning, and should be exposed to the heat a few moments before the rice is put in. The writer claims that "the beverage is equal to the best coffee ever drunk!"—Porcher, *Resources, 580*

SUBSTITUTE FOR COFFEE. The seeds of grapes are very generally used in Germany as a substitute for coffee, and they make an excellent substitute. When pressed, they yield a quantity of oil, and afterwards, when boiled, furnish a liquid very similar to that of coffee. Its flavor is delicious.—*Field and Fireside*, August 8, 1863

RYE COFFEE VS. RIO—HOW TO MAKE THE FORMER. To the Editor: Take Rye, boil it, but not so much as to burst the grain; then dry it, either in the sun, on the stove, or [in] a kiln, after which it is ready for parching, to be used like the real Coffee Bean. Prepared in this manner, it can hardly be distinguished from the genuine Coffee. The Rye when boiled and dried, will keep for any length of time, so as to have it ready whenever wanted for parching.—F. W. Claussen, *Charleston Mercury*, February 8, 1862

SWEET POTATO COFFEE. Peel sweet potatoes and cut to a size of coffee beans. Spread in the sun until perfectly dry. Then parch in an oven or pan until thoroughly brown before being ground. As much as is to be used is then put into a cup with a little hot or cold water. It is mixed well until all is wet, boiling water is added, and it is settled like coffee.—Porcher, *Resources, 400*

AN EXCELLENT SUBSTITUTE FOR COFFEE. For a family of seven or eight persons, take a pint of well roasted corn meal and add to it as much water as an ordinary-sized coffee pot will hold, then boil it well. We have tried this toasted meal coffee and prefer it. Many people cannot drink coffee with impunity, and we advise all such to try the receipt. They will find it more nutritious than coffee and quite as palatable. This is from a correspondent of the *Raleigh Register.*—Porcher, *Resources, 552*

SORGHO SUCRE. I have found from experiments I have made that the seed of the sugar cane (Sorgho Sucre), parched and ground as coffee, prepared in the usual way, but by being boiled a little longer makes an excellent substitute for coffee. My own impression is that, if it were brought into general use, thousands would adopt its use, instead of coffee, even if coffee should again be offered at its former lower prices, from the fact that all could grow and cultivate it with so little labor, and from its approaching so near *the best Java.—Yorkville Enquirer*, January 21, 1863

A SUBSTITUTE FOR COFFEE. The preparation consists simply of the common English pea, picked from the vine when dry, and roasted to a dark cinnamon brown. The taste, says the *Savannah Republican*, is slightly pungent and most palatable, and we would not turn on our heel to exchange it for the genuine article. Try it.—*Albany Patriot*, June 30, 1864

CHINQUAPIN COFFEE. According to the *Augusta Constitutionalist*, chinquapins are said to be a very fair substitute for coffee.—*Yorkville Enquirer*, September 30, 1863

PERSIMMON COFFEE. Save the seeds of the persimmon after they have been boiled, and you let out the slop; for they are excellent for coffee, rather stronger and rougher than the genuine Rio; hence I mix two parts of dried potatoes to one of persimmon seeds. . . . By the boiling the seeds are rid of all mucilaginous substances and just right for coffee or buttons. If you use them for buttons, the washerwoman will hardly break them with her battling stick. For coffee, they should be parched twice as long as any other substitute, so as to make them tender in the centre.—*Confederate Baptist*, November 18, 1863

TO SETTLE COFFEE. The skin of cod-fish, nicely scraped, washed, and dried, is a very good substitute for eggs in settling coffee. A piece the size of a quarter of a dollar will clarify as much as an egg.—*Field and Fireside*, April 2, 1864

SUBSTITUTE FOR CREAM IN COFFEE. Beat the white of an egg to froth. Put to it a small lump of butter and turn the coffee into it gradually so it will not curdle. It is difficult to distinguish from cream.

SUBSTITUTE FOR COFFEE. Okra seeds parched to the right point, and properly drawn, cannot be easily told from the real Java.—*Field and Fireside*, February 6, 1864

HERB AND ROOT TEAS. All herb and root teas should be made with the same care as green tea. Steep them in earthen, tightly closed, and use the drinks while fresh. Most nurses imagine herb teas are boiled herbs. The infusions lose life as readily as green tea by long steeping and exposure to air. Strain the teas before taking them to the patients, and do not let it become insipidly flat before it reaches them.—*Southern Cultivator*, August 1861

DOMESTIC TEA. Cenonothus Americanus, New Jersey tea—called by the country people Yellow Root—grows abundantly in every district in the state. Dry the leaves in the shade and use a little more than of the green tea. I have used this tea for the last two months. It is the best substitute for black tea that I have met with.—*Charleston Tri-Weekly Courier*, June 26, 1862

A SUBSTITUTE FOR HYSON TEA—DELICIOUS TEA. Ladies, gather your raspberry leaves and you will have the finest substitute for hyson tea in the world—and when you can't get raspberries—take the blackberry—it will do. I have tried it.—*Clarke's Confederate Household Almanac*, 1863

SASSAFRAS BLOSSOM AS A SUBSTITUTE FOR BLACK TEA. It is said that if the blossom of the sassafras (which will now soon be in full bloom) be gathered and dried in the shade, be used in making tea, instead of the root, it will be found an excellent substitute for tea, which now sells at from twelve to fifteen dollars a pound.—*Yorkville Enquirer*, April 15, 1863

SMALL BEER. Nine quarts of boiling water, three pints of bran, and a few hops. Strain and cool to milk-warm, then put in a few raisins, one pint of molasses, let stand overnight, strain and bottle.

BEER NO. 2. Two gallons of boiling water, one pint of yeast, three-quarters of a pound of sugar, one ounce of cream of tartar, one of ginger, and cloves to your taste.—*Farmer and Planter*, January 1861

SORGHO BEER. A friend informs us that good beer can be made from the crushed stalks, or "bagasse," of Chinese sugar cane as follows: Take the stalks, after grinding, pack as closely as possible into a barrel or cask; pour on enough water to cover them; place on them a heavy rock, or other weight, to keep them down; and after fermenting three or four days, you have an excellent beer—superior, our informant says, to that made from persimmons. *Try it.*—*Southern Cultivator*, September–October 1863

CORN BEER. Take one pint of corn and boil it soft. Add a pint of molasses and one gallon of water. Shake well and set by the fire, and in twenty-four hours the beer will be excellent. When all the beer in the jug is used up, just add more molasses and water. The same corn will answer for six months, and the beer will be fit for use in twelve hours by keeping the jug where it is warm. In this way, the ingredients used in making a gallon of beer, will cost about $1, and it is better and more wholesome than cider. A little yeast greatly forwards the working of the beer.—*Field and Fireside,* April 11, 1863

MOLASSES BEER, A PLEASANT DRINK. Take a half gallon of molasses (syrup will not do) and mix well with a large tablespoon of best ground ginger and five gallons of water. In two or three days (according to the weather) it will be ready for use. Try it, you that are fond of beer.—*Edgefield Advertiser,* April 20, 1861

SPRUCE BEER. Take three gallons of water, of blood warmth, three half pints of molasses, a tablespoonful of essence of spruce, and a like quantity of ginger—mix together with a gill of yeast. Let stand over night and bottle in the morning. It will be in good condition to drink in twenty-four hours. It is a palatable, wholesome beverage.—*Edgefield Advertiser,* May 22, 1861

CREAM BEER. A correspondent states this makes an effervescing drink far pleasanter than soda water, inasmuch as you do not have to drink for your life in order to get *your money's worth.* The effervescing is much more slow. Take two ounces tartaric acid, two pounds white sugar, the juice of half a lemon, and three pints of water. Boil together five minutes. When nearly cold, add the whites of three eggs well beaten with a cup of flour, and a half ounce of essence of wintergreen. Bottle and keep in a cool place. Take two tablespoonfuls of this syrup for a tumbler of water, and add one quarter of a tablespoonful of soda.—*Edgefield Advertiser,* April 13, 1864

PERSIMMON BEER. The following, which is Mr. Jefferson's recipe for making beer, is the best: Take one bushel of ripe persimmons, mashed and strained, and one-half bushel of wheat bran. Mix well together and bake in loaves of convenient size. Break them in a clean barrel and add twelve gallons of water and two or three ounces of hops. Keep the barrel in a warm room. As soon as fermentation subsides, bottle off the beer, having good long corks, and place the bottles in a low temperature, and it will keep and improve for twelve months. This beer, when properly made in a warm room, is an exquisitely delightful beverage, containing no alcohol, and is, to the connoisseur of temperate taste, not inferior to the fermented juice of the vine.—*Southern Cultivator,* March 1861

PERSIMMON BEER—A SIMPLE METHOD. Put a layer of straw in the bottom of a cask, on which a sufficient quantity of fruit, well mashed, is laid, and the cask then filled with water. It should stand in a warm room, and if the weather is cold, fermentation will be promoted by occasionally putting a warm brick or stone in the barrel. The addition of a few honey locusts, roasted sweet potatoes, or apple peelings, will make the beer more brisk. Wheat bran always improves the quality.

CHINA-BRIAR BEER. The roots of this plant contain a good deal of starch. They are, consequently, to a certain extent, light and porous and are

JOHN HAMMOND MOORE

used to make pipes with, also by our soldiers in camp the manufacture of an extemporaneously prepared beer. The root is mixed with molasses and water in an open tub, a few seeds of parched corn or rice added, and after a slight fermentation it is seasoned with sassafras tea. The young shoots of the China-Briar are eaten as asparagus, with which they are closely allied. They impart the same odor as the urine and probably contain *asparagine.* —Porcher, *Resources,* 387

BLACKBERRY WINE. A patriotic lady, who has been making wine for the soldiers (God bless her!), furnishes the *Athens Banner* with the mode she adopts. Instead of following the old plan of squeezing it with the hand and straining it through cloth, she takes a keg, sets it upon the end, puts straw in the bottom, and after pouring the berries in, pounds them with a wooden pestle, and the juice comes out the hole in the bottom of the keg, perfectly strained and pure. She is of the opinion that the pure juice will keep without sugar, and she is putting up some that way. There should be no water used in making; the wine ferments as usual. Others think that a pound to the gallon is necessary to preserve it. Our readers may act upon their own judgement. If the wine should sour, however, it will make good vinegar, which will be almost as valuable as wine.—*Edgefield Advertiser,* June 15, 1864

BLACKBERRY CORDIAL—FOR SICKNESS IN THE ARMY. To alleviate the suffering and perhaps save the lives of many of our soldiers, whose sickness may be traced to the use of unwholesome water in limestone regions, such as Corinth, I recommend the use of blackberry cordial, and advise all families to make each from one bottle to half a dozen, and send them to the hospitals there. The following is a good recipe: Bruise the berries and strain the juice through a bag. To each quart of juice allow a half pound of loaf sugar, a heaped teaspoonful of powdered cinnamon, the same of powdered cloves, and a grated nutmeg. Boil these ingredients fifteen to twenty minutes, skimming them well. When cool, stir into each quart a pint of brandy, then bottle and cork well. In case brandy and loaf sugar cannot be had, substitute good whiskey and sugar-house molasses. Avoid plantation molasses, brown sugar, and bad whiskey. So much for the cure.

To *prevent* the disorder, boil the water of the country before drinking it. The process of boiling precipitates the impurities, and, when cool, the water may be poured from the sediment and used.—*Edgefield Advertiser,* July 8, 1862

CHERRY CORDIAL. Method of making cherry cordial by the Southern matrons of the lower country South Carolina (St. John's)—a most delectable drink at all times, but particularly valuable in the present emergency: Fill the vessel with cherries (not washed, if gathered clean). Cover with whiskey. After several weeks pour off all the clear liquor and press the cherries through a sieve. Put into the juice thus pressed out, five pints of brown sugar,

THE CONFEDERATE HOUSEWIFE

and boil with syrup enough to sweeten the whole demijohn. Pour five pints of water on the thick part; boil and strain to make the syrup for the sugar. Blackberry cordial is made the same way; or it can be stewed, strained, sweetened, and whiskey added. In the above, the sugar is to be boiled in the water which is obtained from the thick part, as directed.—Porcher, *Resources*, 171

CHAMPAGNE. Of good white wine, take one quart, four ounces of white sugar, a quarter ounce of bicarbonate soda, and one-eighth ounce of tartaric acid. Dissolve the sugar and the acid in the wine and then add the soda. Immediately stop and invert the bottle. In two hours it will be ready for use.— *Field and Fireside*, September 21, 1861

HAVE SOME MADERIA, MY DEAR

Charleston is celebrated for its Maderia, which is always kept in the garrets at the top of the house to ripen, and never in the cellar. It is hardly considered drinkable until it has been twenty years in the bottle, but then it is delicious.

—Ross, *"A Visit,"* 152

SECESSION DRINK. The *Petersburg (Va.) Express* reports a popular restaurant in that city has concocted a drink called the "secession trump." It is made up of an equal proportion of brandy and sherry wine, well mixed with small pieces of lemon and orange, and flavored with a few grains of gunpowder. It is quite palatable, and very popular. When Virginia secedes, a few sprigs of mint are to be added, and this, it is thought, will greatly improve the taste of "secession trump."—*Charleston Mercury*, March 15, 1861

MULLED WINE. Beat together an egg, a glass of wine, and a spoonful of sugar. Pour on it a half a pint of water. Stir all the time to keep it firm, and when you pour into a tumbler, grate a little nutmeg over it.—*Field and Fireside*, January 31, 1863

TO MAKE PURE WINE OF APPLES. Take pure cider made from sound ripe apples as it runs from the press. Put sixty pounds of brown sugar into fifteen gallons of the cider and let it dissolve. Put the mixture into a clean barrel, and fill the barrel up to within two gallons of being full with clean cider.

JOHN HAMMOND MOORE

Put the cask in a cool place, leaving the bung out for forty-eight hours. Then put in the bung, allowing a small vent until fermentation wholly ceases, when bung up tight. In one year, the wine will be fit for use. This wine requires no racking, the longer it stands upon the lees the better.—*Field and Fireside*, August 8, 1863

TOMATO WINE. Take ripe tomatoes, press and strain them, and, to one quart of juice, add one-half pint of sugar. Bottle and let stand until it ferments, when it is ready for use.—*Field and Fireside*, September 20, 1862

EGG NOGG. The following recipe may be a little too tantalizing under the prevailing scarcity of good brandy and sugar, but those who are fortunate enough to have the articles on hand may have a delicious egg nogg by adopting the following directions: Six eggs, whites and yolks beaten separately, very light; six moderate tablespoonfuls of powdered loaf sugar beaten with yolks; mix in whites gradually, adding six tablespoonfuls of good brandy, a little grated nutmeg, and a tumbler of fresh cream. If you have no cream, the same quantity of good rich milk will answer.—*Field and Fireside*, February 7, 1863

SUBSTITUTE FOR LEMONADE. Take the pulp of the pomegranate and stew with white sugar, making a strong syrup. Strain to free it of seeds and bottle for use. A tablespoonful of the syrup in a glass of water, sweetened to the taste, makes a pleasant drink.—*Field and Fireside*, September 20, 1862

SPLENDID SUMMER DRINK. Boil two pounds of mean tobacco in twelve gallons of water; add one bushel of mashed sour apples, and a pint of vitriol—and you have a No. 1 article of whiskey—much superior to any now on the market. This is an old receipt which many have *profitably* used.—*Tri-Weekly Watchman*, August 3, 1863

TO COOL WATER. If it is desired to cool water for drinking in warm weather and ice cannot be had for the purpose, let it be kept in an unglazed, earthenware pitcher, wrapped around with two or three folds of coarse cotton kept constantly wet. The theory of cooling the water in this manner is the absorption of heat from it by evaporation of the moisture in the cotton cloth—expansion produces cold; compression heat.—*Field and Fireside*, April 20, 1861

Soups

TO MAKE SOUP. Soups are never to be filled up or have even a drop of water, hot or cold, added, and are never to boil briskly. They are to be long over the fire, simmering rather than boiling. And all soups having roots or herbs are to have the meat laid on the bottom of the pan, with a good lump of butter. The herbs and roots being cut small, are laid on the meat. It is then covered close and set on a very slow fire. This draws out all the virtue of the roots and herbs, and turns out a good gravy, with a fine flavor, from what it would be if the water were put on first. When the gravy is almost dried up, then fill up the pan with water, and when it begins to boil, "take off" the fat. —*McLeod Journal*

POTABLE SOUP CAKES. Take four pounds of calves' feet, twelve pounds of leg of beef, four pounds of veal knuckle, and ten pounds of leg of mutton. These are to be boiled, the scum taken off as usual. After which the soup is to be separated from the meat by straining and pressure. The meat is then to be boiled a second time in other water, and the two decoctions being added together, must be left to cool, in order that the fat may be exactly separated. The soup must then be clarified with five or six whites of eggs and some table salt added. The liquor is then strained through flannel and evaporated to the consistency of thin paste, after which it is spread on a smooth stone or marble slab. Cut it thin in cakes and dry in a stove until it becomes brittle. Herbs may be boiled with the meats to flavor. It will keep in well closed jars for four or five years. An ounce will make two gallons of good soup.—*Southern Cultivator*, November–December 1862. [Similar recipes often use the word "portable," meaning the dried substance may be carried about; however, "potable" may be intentional—a cake made "drinkable" by adding water.]

NEW FOOD FOR SOLDIERS. A new kind of food for army use, called the extract of flesh, is highly recommended to invalid soldiers and others. A half ounce represents the whole amount of nutriment in a pound of fresh beef. The method of preparation is thus described: The whole process consists in taking lean beef, free of bone and fat, chopping it fine as when used for sausages or mince meat, and mixing it with its own weight of water. It is then slowly heated to boiling and allowed to boil briskly, for a moment or two, when it is strained through cotton cloth to separate the coagulated albumen and fibrin. The evaporation to dryness of the solution must be conducted at a low temperature by a water bath or a steam heat. The powder is readily soluble in water. When properly dried, it will keep for months. Enough can be stored in an ordinary watch fob to sustain a soldier for a week. An ordinary, porcelain-lined kettle, holding a gallon, is sufficient for the preparation of the extract. To dry the solution, put the kettle into a larger vessel containing hot water. But with little trouble on the part of their friends, almost every soldier might be provided with some of this valuable nutriment.—*Southern Cultivator,* January–February 1863

POTATO SOUP

It is but disguised hot water, but like vice, though first abhorred on that account, its victims finally end by preferring it to any thing else. Alice dined out the other day and had all kinds of delicious things to eat, but she confessed to having given a sigh for potato soup, and she declared she had been so long debarred from luxuries she found she could not enjoy them! but to the receipt—a small piece of beef or a little piece of bacon two inches square—hot water—potatoes peeled and boiled in it, and then taken out and passed through the colander, and re-added—seasoned with herbs, pepper and salt, any scraps of vegetables I think should be an improvement.

—Harriott in Flat Rock to her cousin Susan in Columbia, March 10, 1864, in Leland, ed., "Middleton Correspondence," 41.

Nine days later, Susan thanked Harriott for the receipt, adding, "We have not had potatoes for months, and regard them as a first class luxury, entirely beyond our reach."

BROTH FOR THE SICK. Put two pounds of lean beef, one pound of scrag of veal, one pound of scrag of mutton, sweet herbs, and ten peppercorns into a saucepan with five quarts of water. Simmer to three quarts and clear off the fat when cold. Add one onion, if approved. Soup or broth made of different meats is more supporting, as well as better flavored. To remove the fat, take it off when cold, as clean as possible. If there be still any remaining, lay a bit of clean blotting paper on the broth when in the basin, and it will pick up every particle. Or,

THE CONFEDERATE HOUSEWIFE

if the broth is wanted before there is time to let it get cold, put a piece of cork up the narrow end of a funnel, pour the broth into it, let it stand for a few minutes, and the fat will rise to the top. Remove the cork and draw off into a basin as much of the broth as is wanted, which will be perfectly free of fat.—*Field and Fireside*, January 10, 1863

LIGHT BREAD SOUP. Boil in a saucepan a pint of water, to which add an egg well beaten, two slices of bread, toasted brown, a teacup of sweet milk, and a little butter. Heat and salt and pepper to taste.—*Field and Fireside*, January 31, 1863

A POOR MAN'S SOUP. Mince a handful of parsley leaves fine and steam over a little salt. Shred six green onions and put them with the parsley in a saucepan. Add three tablespoonfuls of oil and vinegar, with some pepper and salt. Pour over it a nice beef broth, and it is ready to serve.—*Field and Fireside*, February 7, 1863

To Our Soldiers.

You may rest assured there is a deal of contrivance, and forethought, and prudence, now exerted in the South, to produce meat as well as bread in abundance. Every man knows every hog he owns and can identify it a hundred yards off running through a pine-thicket. He not only knows it, but he pets it and feeds it, and comes very near washing and combing it into sleekness of proportion and abundancy of size. The like of bacon was never known in America as will be forth-coming from this high-pressure system of hog-economy. But it will be needed, and no man should relax his care and attention in the matter for a single day.

—Edgefield Advertiser, June 25, 1862.

JOHN HAMMOND MOORE

Bread, Crackers, &c.

BUYING FLOUR. It is about as difficult a job to buy good flour as to buy a good horse. Let us tell you how to go to work with it. First, look at color. If it is white, with a slightly yellowish or straw-colored tint, buy it. If it is very white, with a bluish cast, or with black specks in it, refuse it. Second, examine the adhesiveness; wet and knead a little of it between your fingers. If it works soft and sticky, it is poor. Flour from spring wheat is likely to be very sticky. Third, throw a lump of dry flour against a dry, smooth, perpendicular surface. If it falls to the floor, it is bad. Fourth, squeeze some of the flour in your hand. If it retained the shape given by the pressure, this, too, is a good sign. Flour that will stand all these tests is safe to buy.—*Camden Daily Journal*, October 8, 1864

PRACTICAL DIRECTIONS FOR MAKING BREAD. To the Editor: As most of the ingredients for raising bread, such as yeast powders, &c. are becoming scarce, I think a good receipt given to housekeepers not out of the way: Take about eight or ten middling-sized Irish potatoes, pare and cut them fine; then set them to cook, with about three times as much water as will cover them. When done, mash them fine in the same water, then add flour enough to make a thick batter. Remember the flour must be put in while the water is boiling hot; let it cool off until about lukewarm, and then add a little piece of sour dough, say a teaspoonful to start with. Of course, after the house-keeper has once made this yeast, she can always keep a little of the old to add to the new. If kept in a warm place, it will be fit for use in about six hours. Add plenty of this to your flour, and you will have the lightest and best tasted [sic] bread that you could wish for. F. W. Claussen, Claussen Mills.—*Charleston Mercury*, January 31, 1862

NEW YEAST. As hops are very scarce, I yesterday tried the following: Take a double handful of hoarhound leaves. Boil them in a gallon of water. Stir in a pint of flour while boiling and add when cold a large spoonful of brown sugar, a little salt, and a gill of old yeast. It makes a yeast as well as hops and keeps better. Take a teacupful of this yeast and two quarts of flour to make a family loaf.—*Field and Fireside*, May 17, 1862

GOOD YEAST. Take a half pint of corn meal and make into a batter with equal parts of sweet milk and warm water; then add a large spoonful of brown sugar and a little yeast. When well risen, add corn meal sufficient to make it almost dry; then spread on a large dish and put in the shade to dry. Keep in a close bag. One handful is the quantity to be used when you make up bread.—*Tri-Weekly Watchman*, April 13, 1863

PEACH LEAF YEAST. Hops cost two dollars per pound, leaves cost nothing, and peach leaves make better yeast than hops. Thus: Take three handfuls of peach leaves and three medium-sized potatoes, boil them in two quarts of water until the potatoes are done, take out the leaves, and rub them up with a pint of flour, adding cool water sufficient to make a paste, then pour on the hot peach leaf tea, and scald for about five minutes. If you add to this a little old yeast, it will be ready for use in three hours. If you add none, it will require to stand a day and a night before use. Leaves dried in the shade are as good as fresh ones. As this is stronger than hop yeast, less should be used in making up the dough.—*Camden Daily Journal*, July 12, 1864

TO MAKE DIFFERENT KINDS OF BREAD WITH RICE FLOUR

LOAF RICE BREAD. Boil a pint of rice soft, add a pint of leaven, then three quarts of rice flour. Put it to rise in a tin or earthen vessel. When it has risen sufficiently, divide it into three parts and bake it as other bread, and you will have three large loaves. Or scald the flour and, when cold, mix half wheat flour or corn meal, raised with leaven in the same way. Another—take one quart of rice flour and make it into a stiff pap by wetting with water, as much as two or three quarts. Stir it constantly until it boils. Put in one-half pint of yeast when it cools, add a little salt, knead in as much wheat flour as will make it a proper dough for bread, put it to rise, and when risen add a little more wheat flour. Let it stand in a warm place half an hour, and then bake it. This same mixture, only made thinner and baked in rings, makes excellent muffins.

JOURNEY OR JOHNNY CAKES. To three spoonfuls of soft boiled rice, add a small teacup of water or milk. Then add six spoonfuls of the rice flour, which will make a johnny cake or six waffles.

RICE CAKES. Take a pint of soft boiled rice, a half pint of milk or water, to which add twelve spoonfuls of rice flour. Divide into small cakes and bake them in a brick oven.

RICE CAKES LIKE BUCKWHEAT CAKES. Mix one-fourth wheat flour to three-fourths superfine rice flour. Raise it as buckwheat flour and bake like buckwheat cakes.

TO MAKE RICE WAFERS. Take a pint of warm water, a teaspoonful of salt, and a pint of flour, and it will give you a dozen wafers.

TO MAKE RICE PUFFS. To a pint of the flour add a teaspoonful of salt and a pint of boiling water. Beat up four eggs and stir them well together with the mixture. Put from two to three spoonfuls of lard in a pan, make it boiling hot, and fry as you would common fritters.

RICE GRIDDLE CAKES. Boil one large cup of whole rice quite soft in milk and, while hot, stir in a little wheat flour or rice flour. When cold, add two eggs and a little salt and bake in small thin cakes on a griddle.

Note. In every case in making rice flour bread, cake, or pudding, a well boiled pap should be first made of all the milk and water and half the flour, and allowed to get perfectly cold before the other ingredients are added. It forms a support for them and prevents the flour from settling at the bottom. Stir the whole a moment before it is set to cook.—*Clarke's Confederate Household Almanac,* 1863

REMEMBERING AUNT BETTY'S BREADS

She had more kinds of bread than any woman I ever heard of; splendid, hot, high, light bread—the best bread of all others; if I am a judge—and rolls, and biscuit, and waffles, and batter cakes, and muffins, and pone, and ash-cake, and hoe-cake, and "salt risen" bread, and apple-bread, and cracklin bread—did you ever eat any cracklin bread?—and many others; to say nothing of fritters, and pan-cakes, and suet-dumplings, and things of that sort.

—Southern Literary Messenger, May 1863, 304

SECESSION RICE BREAD. Take one pint and a half of rice flour, three gills of milk, three eggs, a tablespoonful of butter, a teaspoonful of salt, a salt-spoonful of carbonate of soda, and rather less of tartaric acid. Beat up well and bake in a quick oven. Add the tartaric last. The mixture should be the consistency of cake before baking.—*McLeod Journal*

A RICH CORN BREAD. Take two quarts of corn meal, one quart wheat flour, a little salt, and four eggs. Add enough buttermilk to form a stiff batter. Mix well, then add two teaspoonfuls of soda dissolved in a little warm water.

Stir and pour into greased pans, so that it will be about two inches thick when baked. Bake in a hot oven until done—say about half an hour.—*Field and Fireside,* January 31, 1863

SNOW CORN CAKES. Take any desired quantity of Indian meal and add sugar and salt to taste. Stir in with a spoon two or three times its bulk of snow. Try a little on a hot griddle. If it cooks too dry to turn well, add more snow. If too wet to be light, add more meal. Bake like buckwheat cakes.—*Edgefield Advertiser,* January 7, 1863

CELEBRATED INDIAN BREAD AS PREPARED AT THE ST. CHARLES HOTEL, NEW ORLEANS. Beat two eggs very light, mix alternately with them one pint of sour milk or buttermilk and one pint of fine Indian meal. Melt a tablespoonful of butter and add to the mixture. Also, add a tablespoonful of soda or saleratus, etc., dissolved in a small portion of the milk, and beat very hard. Bake in a pan in a quick oven.—*Field and Fireside,* April 18, 1863

SALLY LUNN. I am tempted to send my recipe for this most delicious tea bread, which, once eaten at your table, will cause your friends to rejoice when asked to come again. Take a stone pot, pour in one pint of sweet milk, half a teacup of baker's or other yeast, one quarter of a pound of melted butter, a little salt, and three beaten eggs. Mix in about three pint bowls of flour. Let it stand several hours, or until quite light, then put into Turk-heads or other tin pans, in which Sally should again rise up before being shoved into the oven, to be "brought out and presented to your friends as the beauty and belle of the evening."—*Southern Cultivator,* January–February 1863

SALLY LUNN—THE EASY WAY. One quart of flour, three eggs, three tablespoonfuls of sugar, one tablespoonful of butter, no particular quantity of milk, only enough to make the batter as stiff as you can beat it. Bake as usual.

BROWN BREAD. One quart of rye meal, two quarts of Indian meal, and two tablespoonfuls of molasses. Mix thoroughly with sweet milk, let stand for one hour, and then bake in a slow oven.—*Field and Fireside,* April 11, 1863

SAGO BREAD. This light and nutritious article for invalids is made in the following manner: Soak two pounds of sago in water or milk for several hours. Then mix with as much flour and add saleratus and good yeast (and a little Indian meal, if liked). When well raised, give it a handsome bake. It is delicious, healthy, and cheap.—*Field and Fireside,* February 13, 1864

COFFEE CAKES. Take some rice that has been boiled soft, twice as much flour as rice, a little Indian meal, and a little yeast. Mix with cold water and let rise overnight. This will make fine biscuits for breakfast.

CRUMPETS. Put a half gill of yeast into a quart of warm water with a teaspoon of salt. Stir in flour enough to make a pretty stiff batter and set in a warm place to rise. When light add a cup of melted butter and bake as muffins.

JOHN HAMMOND MOORE

INDIAN SPONGE BREAD. Three eggs, one pint of buttermilk, one pint of corn meal, one teaspoonful of soda. Mix and bake in a quick oven.—*Field and Fireside*, February 14, 1863

INDIAN FLAP-JACKS. Scald a quart of Indian meal—when luke-warm, stir in half a pint of flour, half a teacup of yeast, and a little salt. When light, fry them in just enough fat to prevent their sticking to the frying-pan. Another method of making them, which is very nice, is to turn boiling milk or water on the Indian meal, in the proportion of a quart of the former to a pint of the latter—stir in three tablespoonfuls of flour, three eggs well beaten, and a couple teaspoonfuls of salt.—*Clarke's Confederate Household Almanac*, 1863

FRITTERS QUICKLY MADE. One egg, two spoonfuls of flour, a little sifted sugar and ginger mixed with milk sufficient to make a smooth batter. Cut a middling-sized apple into thick slices and put into the batter, and with a spoon put them into the frying pan with just the batter which is taken up in the spoon. Have a sieve with the bottom up, and, as fried, lay the fritters upon it to drain. This quantity is sufficient for a small dish.—*McLeod Journal*

HOMINY CAKES. A pint of grits boiled soft—add salt, beat in thoroughly one egg and two spoonfuls of wheat flour. Drop with a spoon and fry in cakes.—*Edgefield Advertiser*, March 1, 1863

HOMINY BREAD. The hominy having been properly soaked, drain off the water and add of fresh water seven and one-half pints for each pound and a half of hominy, as weighed before soaking. Let this simmer for four hours—if boiled rapidly, it will become hard and never swell. The hominy then will be fit for stirabout or bread. For bread, mix it gradually with flour, making the dough in the ordinary way, and adding yeast in rather more than the usual proportion. This bread will keep moist and good for a longer time than if made entirely of wheaten flour.—*Field and Fireside*, January 10, 1863

BUCKWHEAT BREAD. To make buckwheat bread or johnny cake, add a teaspoonful of soda to one quart of buttermilk and enough flour to make a thin batter. Put in an egg, if convenient, and bake in a quick oven. Try it.—*Field and Fireside*, January 18, 1863

SAVE YOUR OLD BREAD. Every person may not know what, however, is true. Pieces of old bread, crumbs, &c., being soaked and mixed up with dough, in making new bread, improves it very much. Try it, and you will never allow pieces of any bread to be lost afterward—especially when flour is selling for fifty dollars per barrel.—*Field and Fireside*, March 7, 1863

RUSK. Take at night one teacup of milk, half a cup of butter, one teacup of fresh yeast, and two eggs. Beat all together and add enough flour to make a very stiff dough. In the morning, add sugar and cinnamon to taste and a little more flour, to have it about the consistency of loaf bread. Knead well. Let it rise again and bake with gradual heat.—*Field and Fireside*, February 14, 1863

POTATO WAFERS. When flour is so high priced as at present, sweet potatoes can be used to great advantage in a variety of breads. Boil two large or four smaller sweet potatoes. Peel and mash them. Put in a large spoonful of lard, a little salt, and knead into them half a pound of wheat flour. Cut into small pieces and bake in a waffle iron, or roll out thin, cut into squares, and bake in an oven as biscuits. A little milk—an egg—or one or two tablespoonfuls of sugar may be added—at will or possession, but simply made as above they are excellent tea cakes.—*Edgefield Advertiser*, March 1, 1863

SWEET POTATO WAFFLES. Two tablespoonfuls of mashed potatoes, one of butter, one of sugar, one pint of milk, and four tablespoonfuls of wheat flour. Mix well and bake in a waffle iron.

RAISED WAFFLES. Make a thick batter of milk and wheat flour, add four eggs, beat light a gill of yeast, a spoonful of butter; let it rise some hours.—*Field and Fireside*, March 21, 1863

To Our Soldiers

To remedy the scarcity [of wheat], you may be informed that our house-keepers generally are making a brave old use of the sweet potato. Mixed meal and potato biscuit, with a dash of flour, is no bad victuals, with a little Confederate coffee to wash it down,—and by Confederate coffee we mean any warm drink whatever, from a "sassifax" up to rye oh!, moderately sweetened with coarse brown sugar.

—Edgefield Advertiser, February 18, 1863

TO MAKE CRACKERS. Take one egg, one pint of sweet milk, one teacupful of lard, a little salt, and enough flour to make a stiff dough. Rub the lard and some flour together; then add the egg and milk. Add flour and knead well till it is a very stiff dough. Add to this one-half of its size a light dough, knead well together, and set aside to rise. When light, roll out to one-eighth of an inch thick, cut in squares, prick with a fork, and bake to a crisp.—*Field and Fireside*, January 17, 1863

BUTTER CRACKERS. Four eggs, one cup of sour cream, a lump of butter the bigness of an egg, flour sufficient to knead good. Pound ten minutes, then roll out, cut in squares, and bake.—*Field and Fireside,* June 27, 1863

I Am Obliged to Economize in Cooking

Atlanta, March 14, 1863—Have been busy baking bread, pies, and cake. Did not have much success with any thing. Every thing is so high that I am obliged to economize in cooking—can not make things as palateable as I would like. Prices continue to rise. Flour is now $75 per barrel. Irish potatoes $20 a bushel. Rice flour $20 per hundred. Corn meal $3 per bushel. Bacon $1 per pound. Beef 50 cts per pound. The last two articles are beyond our reach. We use rye as a substitute for coffee. Sylvanus bought 1/4 lb. of tea and occasionally we treat ourselves to a cup of the refreshing beverage.

—Jennie Akehurst Diary

Milk, Butter, Cheese & Eggs

MILKING COWS. It is a matter of great importance that the milk should all be drawn from the cow's udder. Careful experiments show that the quantity of cream obtained from the last drawn cup, from most cows, exceeds that of the first in a proportion of twelve to one. Thus a person who carelessly leaves but a teacupful of milk withdrawn, loses in reality about as much cream as he would be afforded by four or six pints in the beginning, and loses, too, that part of the cream which gives the richness and high flavor to the butter.—*Southern Enterprise,* July 1, 1861

TO DIVEST MILK AND BUTTER OF THE TASTE OF TURNIPS. Put into each pail of milk, when freshly drawn from the cows, one pint of boiling water. The heat of the water dispels the odor of the turnip, which becomes volatile as the temperature of the milk is increased.—*Southern Recorder,* September 8, 1863

PRESERVING MILK. Place new milk in a clean pot and evaporate until nothing remains but a light, dry powder. Put this in a bottle and seclude it carefully from the air by corking and waxing. When milk is wanted, dissolve a small quantity in pure, soft water. The solution will be found to possess the qualities, as well as the familiar taste and aroma of milk freshly drawn from the cow.—*Field and Fireside,* August 8, 1863

TO PRESERVE BUTTER. Take the ears of corn carefully from the shuck so as to leave the latter all joined together. Put the shuck into boiling water until soft, then throw into cold water. Have the butter well worked and fill up the shuck, enclosing it in the same manner that the corn was. Tie the ends firmly, packing each one into a jar and covering them well with salt and water.—*Field and Fireside,* August 22, 1863

TO MAKE YELLOW BUTTER IN WINTER. For a churning of ten to twelve pounds of butter, take about three or four carrots. Grate fine and pour out the juice. Then pour hot water over them and press again. Take the juice thus obtained and mix with it about a pint of new or sweet milk. Put this into the cream and churn as usual.—*Field and Fireside,* September 20, 1862

CHEESE. By Mrs. E. M. Bobo, Musgrove's Mill. Take a piece of rennet six inches long and three wide, soak it eight hours in a pint and a half of water, adding a tablespoon of salt. Then take five gallons of milk, heated to 95°. Strain the preparation of rennet into the milk, stirring it briskly all the while. Let it stand thirty or forty minutes, until it coagulates, then break the mass into pieces with a knife or spoon, after which the whey will rise. Then gently press it with your hands into a small mass, pour the whey off, and set it by to cool in a basin until morning. Then pick or crumble this curd into pieces the size of a grain of corn, salt it to your taste, lay a cloth on your cheese hoop, put the curd in it, nicely folding the cloth over the top, and putting on it at first a gentle pressure. Turn the curd over every six hours, increasing the pressure each time. Keep it in press forty-eight hours.—*Farmer and Planter,* April 1861

SOUR MILK CHEESE. Heat sour or loppered milk (which is better) in an iron pot over a slow fire, until curd is formed. Take out the curd and press the whey from it with a ladle or the hands. To each quart of curd add one-half pint of sweet cream, a lump of butter the size of an egg, and salt to taste. Place all the ingredients in a frying pan over a slow fire, and stir until it assumes a smooth, thick consistence, when it is ready for the table, either warm or cold. [Some housekeepers place the curd in a strainer bag and allow the whey to drip out, before adding the cream, etc. The second heating appears to be an improvement.—Ed.]—*Southern Cultivator,* January–February 1863

TO MAKE SAGE CHEESE. Take the tops of sage and press the juice from them in a mortar. Do the same with leaves of spinach and mix the two juices together. After putting the rennet in the milk, pour in some of the juice, regulating the quantity by the color and taste to be given the cheese. As the curd appears, break it gently and in an equal manner; then, emptying it into the cheese-vat, let it be a little pressed, in order to make it eat mellow. Having stood for about seven hours, salt and turn it daily for four or five weeks, when it will be fit to eat. The spinach, besides improving the flavor and correcting the bitterness of the sage, will give a much finer color than can be obtained with sage alone.—*Southern Cultivator,* November–December 1862

BRANDY CHEESE. The cheese you had, Mr. Editor, when with us the other day, and of which you wanted the recipe, was packed down in April, 1861, just as the war commenced. To each pound of cheese, well beaten in a mortar, was added a tablespoon of brandy, and both well mixed, then packed down tightly in Arthur's earthen cans and sealed up. The cheese improves for a year and will keep for ten. Mouldy cheese, by having the mould cut out, can thus be preserved; and, even if the cheese is very dry, it may be grated and is just as good as ever if thus put up. All taste and smell of the brandy is lost in keeping.—*Southern Cultivator,* May–June 1863

PRESERVING EGGS. Eggs may be preserved by applying with a brush a solution of gum arabic to the shells, and afterwards packing them in dry charcoal dust.—*Southern Recorder,* June 17, 1862

THE WAY TO KEEP EGGS FRESH. Pack them in small boxes and about once a week turn every box, and they will keep fresh and untainted for an indefinite period. The reason is, by turning the egg over frequently and regu-

THE CONFEDERATE HOUSEWIFE

larly, the yolk is kept about the center of the albumen. If kept still, the yolk will, in a short time, find its way through the white to the shell, and when it does the egg will spoil. Hens understand this fact, for they, as we know, turn over the eggs on which they set at least daily.—*Southern Confederacy*, November 7, 1862

TO PRESERVE EGGS. Provide a small cupboard, safe, or tier of shelves. Bore the shelves full of holes one and one-quarter inches in diameter and place the eggs in them, point downward. They will keep sound for several months. Other modes, such as packing in salt, &c., depend for their success simply in placing the points down. The shelves are more convenient and accessible.—*Field and Fireside*, April 4, 1863

PUFF OMELET. This is very superior, as well as beautiful. Beat the yolks of six eggs light and mix them in a small teacup of milk; add a little salt. Beat together a tablespoonful of sweet butter with the same quantity of flour until smooth; add the mixture to the custard and beat the whole together. Pour it into a butter omelet or a small frying pan, and when it begins to thicken, pour over it the whites, beaten stiff. Dust over it a trifle of salt, and when the whole is stiff, remove it carefully to the dish without breaking.
—*Field and Fireside, June 1, 1861*

LADIES, TAKE NOTICE.

In putting up cooked provisions for soldiers, be sure to let everything become throughly cool before it is boxed up. When put up warm, it will spoil in a few hours, so that it cannot be eaten. Much that has been sent to the forts and camps has been lost on that account.

—*Charleston Daily Courier, July 6, 1861.*

Fruits & Vegetables

PRESERVING WITH CHARCOAL. Apples, beets, potatoes, and carrots may be preserved more than a year if treated as follows: In a cool cellar, place the fruit or vegetables on a bed of pulverized charcoal. Add a layer of charcoal and then more fruit and vegetables alternately until all are disposed of. The coal must be well dried.—*Field and Fireside*, July 11, 1863

TO KEEP APPLES FOR THE WINTER. Put them in casks or bins in layers well covered with dry sand, each layer being covered. This preserves them from the air, from moisture, and from frost; it prevents them perishing from their own perspiration, their moisture being absorbed by the sand; at the same time it preserves the flavor of the apples, and prevents their wilting. Pippins have been kept in this manner sound and fresh till mid-summer, and how much longer they would have kept is not known. Any kind of sand will answer, but it must be perfectly dry.—*Camden Confederate*, October 24, 1862

HOW TO MAKE APPLE BUTTER. Take two barrels of cider made from nice, sound, sweet apples; draw off six or eight gallons; then boil the remainder to syrup. Peel and core five bushels of sweet apples and the same quantity of sour apples. Put the raw cider in the kettle (which should be copper or brass) and boil and skim it; then put in the sweet apples and boil till tender. Dip part of them out and put in the sour ones. Boil a few minutes, then gradually add the apples you took out and the syrup. Boil till smooth; spice to taste. Commence stirring as soon as you put in the apples and continue till done, or it will be very sure to burn fast to the kettle.—*Field and Fireside*, January 26, 1861

ROASTING. An easy mode of roasting potatoes, apples, or eggs, which we publish for the benefit of soldiers and others. Take your potatoes, or whatever you wish to roast, and after washing them clean, wrap them in a paper two or three times over. When this is done, put them in a can of water and squeeze until the paper is wet to the potato. Squeeze them well and make a place in the embers, lay them in, and cover them with hot ashes, with no coals. After they have lain a proper time, take them out and the paper will be found to be perfectly dry and not burnt; and, on opening, the paper will be very hot and damp the nearer you get to the potatoes—and the potatoes will be soft and clean, and will peel much easier and cleaner than when boiled. An Irish potato when boiled loses half of its sweetness, but when prepared in this manner, it does not lose its sweetness, but is better tasting.

Apples, when roasted in this way, are not like what they are when baked, black and burnt, but have a beautiful brown cast. Eggs thus prepared are much better than any other mode of cooking them and will cool in less time than when boiling, if you have hot embers.—*Southern Banner,* July 20, 1864

TO PRESERVE STRAWBERRIES OR RASPBERRIES FOR CREAMS OR ICES WITHOUT BOILING. Let the fruit be gathered in the middle of a warm day, in very dry weather. Strip it off from the stalk directly, weigh it, turn it into a bowl or deep pan, and bruise it gently. Then mix with an equal weight of fine, dry-sifted sugar and immediately put into small, wide-necked bottles. Cork them firmly without delay and tie bladders over the tops. Keep them in a cool place or the fruit will ferment. The mixture should be stirred softly and only just sufficiently to blend the sugar and the fruit. The bottles must be perfectly dry, and the bladders, after having been cleaned in the usual way and allowed to become nearly so, should be moistened with a little spirit on the side which is to be next to the cork.

TO KEEP PRESERVES. Apply the white of an egg, with a suitable brush, to a single thickness of white tissue paper, with which to cover jars, overlapping the edges an inch or two. When dry, the whole will become tight as a drum. To prevent jams, preserves, etc., from graining, a teaspoonful of cream of tartar must be added to every gallon of the jam or preserves.

STRAWBERRIES STEWED FOR TARTS. Make a syrup of one pound of sugar and a teacup of water. Add a little white of an egg, let boil, and skim until only the foam rises. Then put in a quart of berries free from stems and hulls. Let them boil till they look clear and the syrup is quite thick. Finish as directed for tarts, with fine puff paste.

TO PRESERVE STRAWBERRIES IN WINE. Put a quantity of the finest large strawberries into a good sherry bottle and strew over them three large spoonfuls of fine sugar. Fill up with Madeira or sherry.—*Edgefield Advertiser,* May 22, 1861

TO MAKE BRANDY PEACHES. Peel the peaches and scald them in water until they begin to get a little soft. Leave them in a dish all night. Then fill up the jar two-thirds full of peaches and fill it up with rum and let them stand ten days. Then draw off the rum and sweeten it with loaf sugar as long as it will take it. Pour it back in the jar and seal it up.—*McLeod Journal*

DRIED FIGS. Gather when well ripe, preserving the stem. Make a syrup by melting sugar (crushed or loaf is preferable, but brown will do). While hot, dip the fig into the syrup two or three times, and then lay in the sun or place in oven to dry. After the fruit is tolerably dry, cover the bottom of a vessel with fig leaves and sprinkle thereon a slight layer of sugar. Put in a layer of figs, stems uppermost, cover the fruit with a little sugar, and then put in another layer of fruit, and so on until the vessel is filled. After it has stood this way, say forty-eight hours, put a press on the fruit and let it remain until it shall become compressed thoroughly.—*Edgefield Advertiser*, July 23, 1863

A FIG FOR MOLASSES. Wash the figs, then put them in a porcelain vessel. Cover with pure water and boil carefully one hour. When cool, strain through a muslin cloth; then boil down to a proper consistency, which you can easily tell by dipping up a spoonful and cooling. The above is all the preparation necessary. In boiling the last time, take the scum off.—*Yorkville Enquirer,* July 31, 1862

MOLASSES FROM WATERMELONS. Nothing is easier or more simple than to make molasses from the juice of watermelons. Take the juice of ripe melons and boil it in a large pot or kettle, the larger the better, until it is brought to the proper consistence, adding fresh juice from time to time as it boils away. This is all that is necessary, and this anyone can do. If this business is conducted on a large scale, a simple press, similar to the old-fashioned cider press, can be made to extract the juice from the pulp. After being pressed, the pulp should be put in a barrel and left to ferment. Draw off the liquid produced by the fermentation, and it will be found to be the best of vinegar.—*Edgefield Advertiser*, July 23, 1863

BLACKBERRY SYRUP. To two quarts of juice of blackberries, add one pound of loaf sugar, half an ounce of nutmeg, half an ounce of cinnamon, pulverized, one-quarter of an ounce of cloves, one-quarter of an ounce of all-spice, pulverized. Boil together for a short time, and when cold add a pint of fourth-proof French brandy.—*Confederate States Almanac,* 1864

NEW METHOD OF MAKING JELLY. Press the juice from the fruit, add the proper proportion of sugar, and stir the juice and sugar until the sugar is completely melted. Put it into jars, and in twenty-four hours it will be of proper consistence. By this means the trouble of boiling is avoided, and the jelly retains more completely the flavor of the fruit. Care should be taken to stir the mixture until the sugar is completely melted, and fine sugar should be used.—*Southern Enterprise*, April 3, 1861

GENERAL HINTS FOR COOKING VEGETABLES

Sweet potatoes are much better baked than boiled, and in that form are almost as nutritious as bread. Irish potatoes, when new, should be put into boiling water with their skins entire. When the skins crack, they are done enough. They are spoiled by lying in the water after they are cooked. Drain off the water and leave them in the hot kettle to dry.

Onions should be boiled until tender, the water being carefully skimmed.

45

It is very good with a dressing of cream or thickened milk.

Cauliflowers should be soaked an hour in cold water with a handful of salt in it, and then boiled in milk and water, skimming carefully. Serve with the same dressing as cabbage, or with one prepared as follows: Into scalding milk stir a thickening of fine flour in *cold* milk, and when it has simply boiled, add a few beaten eggs, boil a few seconds more and it is ready for use.

Parsnips are not properly appreciated among us. Boil half an hour, or until tender. They are good without any dressing, but are improved by the same treatment as recommended for cauliflower. Cut in slices and browned on a griddle, they are nice.

Carrots should be soaked in cold water before boiling. Boil from half to three-quarters of an hour.

Beets require from one to three hours of boiling, according to age and size.

Guinea squash, or egg plant, should be cut in slices a quarter of an inch thick, sprinkled with salt, and piled on a plate, one side of which must be raised to allow the acrid juice to run off. In half an hour, wash them in fresh water, dip them in a batter of eggs and bread crumbs, and brown on a griddle.

All vegetables should be gathered early, while the dew is still upon them. After being washed, they may be laid in cold water until ready for boiling; then take them out, boil the same water, and when it is at the boiling point, throw them in. Such vegetables as have a strong flavor, like the onion, cabbage, &c., should not, however, be cooked in the same water.—*Southern Cultivator,* April 1861

PORK AND BEANS. Pick over and wash a quart of beans. Soak ten or twelve hours in three quarts of cold water, drain, put in kettle with enough fresh water to cover. When they begin to boil, drain again, and cover with cold water. Lay a bit of pork four inches square over them, cover closely, and boil till tender. Add a teaspoonful of soda or saleratus and a little salt, if the pork has not salted them sufficiently. Stir thoroughly and pour into a bake pan. Cut the rind off the pork into squares, place in center, and bake in moderate hot oven till a fine, crisp, brown crust has formed over the top.—*Field and Fireside,* April 25, 1863

PRESERVING SNAP BEANS. Cut up the beans, taking out the strings, and thus prepare them for the table. Then scald in salt and water and dry on a scaffold like fruits. Others preserve them in salt, like pickles, the bean making its own brine. In either case, the beans are soaked in water before cooking.—*Edgefield Advertiser,* April 27, 1864

THREE DISHES FROM BEETS. Beets, as we all know, are very good and very wholesome, when the roots only are cooked in the ordinary manner, but many do not know that the tops make most excellent salad, rivalling, if not surpassing, Scotch kale. And a still smaller number know that the stem or shank of the leaf, when cut up and cooked as snaps, makes a dish which but very few can tell from the real article.—*Field and Fireside*, July 11, 1863

CABBAGE. Large, full-grown cabbages and savoys will require half an hour or more of boiling. Strip all the outside leaves to the very white ones; then shave the stalk and score it a little way up. Boil with good bacon. Cold cabbage may be fried with ham.—*Field and Fireside*, January 25, 1863

HOT SLAW. Cut a good cabbage and with a sharp knife slice it fine. Put it in a stew pan with a piece of butter, and salt and pepper it to taste. Pour in just hot water enough to keep it from sticking to the pan. Cover closely and let it stew. Stir frequently; and, when it is quite tender, add a little vinegar and serve it hot.—*Southern Cultivator*, August 1861

CABBAGE SALAD. Chop enough cabbage fine to fill a vegetable dish. Heat a coffee cup of strong vinegar, with a lump of butter in it the size of an egg. Add pepper and salt. When hot, beat an egg very light and stir in; then pour all on the chopped cabbage.—*Southern Cultivator*, September–October 1862

CURING GREEN CORN. The following is the Indian method by which they treat green corn for making succotash during the winter. When the green corn is fit for use, a pit is dug from two to three feet in diameter at the top and gradually enlarging at the bottom, say five feet down, from six to eight feet in diameter. A large fire is then built nearby, on which stones are heated, and, when red hot, the stones and live coals are shoveled into the bottom of the pit, and sprinkled over with fine loose dirt. The corn is then thrown in with husks on, just as it is pulled from the stalk, until the pit is nearly full. Then comes a thin layer of loose dirt, then hot stones (enough to close the pit), and the whole covered with earth to retain the heat. When the whole cools off (which takes several days), the pit is opened and the corn is found to be delightfully cooked. When cool, the husks are stripped off, and the corn is dried in the sun. When thoroughly dried, the corn is shelled off easily and is then packed away in bags for use.—*Charleston Tri-Weekly Courier*, August 12, 1862

GREEN CORN PUDDING. Gather the corn in the milk, when neither too young nor too ripe. Shell, cut, or scrap the corn from the cob and pound it fine in a mortar. To four dozen ears, add one pint of milk and half a pound of sugar, the whole to be mixed and baked about two hours, till the crust shows a dark brown color. Eat with fresh butter.—*McLeod Journal*

PRESERVING CORN. Scald the corn about three minutes to coagulate the milk or albuminous portion, then cut it from the cob and spread it on flat dishes. Place them either on a shelf hung over the stove or range or in a very moderate oven. Dry the corn as quickly as possible without scorching, and disturb it frequently with a spoon while drying. Put it away in bags, and in winter soak it a few hours before boiling.—*Edgefield Advertiser,* September 17, 1862

TO PRESERVE CORN FOR BOILING. Pluck the corn when fit for eating—strip away the husk so as to remove the silk and then replace it. Pack away in a barrel and pour on a strong pickle (such as used for meat), with a weight to keep it down, and you will have a good sea-stock. Par-boiled, and then boiled, will make it perfectly fresh and sweet as when taken from the stalk.—*Field and Fireside,* April 4, 1863

BAKED EGG PLANT. This vegetable is usually cut in slices and fried in butter or lard. When cooked in this way, it absorbs too much fat to be easily digested and cannot safely be eaten by those inclined to dyspepsia. We have recently heard of the following method, by which this difficulty is avoided. Let the plants be nearly ripe, cut in halves, and remove part of the middle pulp. Prepare dressing as for stuffing a turkey, fill the plants, put the halves together, and bake them. This is said to make an excellent dish.—*Field and Fireside,* October 4, 1862

HOMINY. Now that meal is hard to get, we recommend lye-hominy as a good substitute for bread, at least as a change. The simple plan for preparing it is as follows: To a gallon of shelled corn add half a gallon of good ashes. Boil together until the husk begins to come off the corn. Then rub briskly to clear the grain completely of husk. Wash the corn clean and boil for ten or twelve hours, adding water from time to time to keep it from burning. It is then ready and has only to be warmed over for use as needed.—*Field and Fireside,* March 14, 1863

DRY HOMINY FOR DINNER

I returned home to find <u>dry hominy</u> the only dinner to be had. . . . Hominy, corn bread & occasionally a little peas or eggs & still more rarely a scrap of bacon, is our ordinary bill of fare.

—*Emma Holmes Diary, May 3, 1864.*

Miss Holmes, a Charlestonian, was teaching school in Camden at this time.

JOHN HAMMOND MOORE

OKRA PUT UP FOR WINTER USE. By Mrs. R. J. Gage, Union. Take a large jar, sprinkle a layer of good salt over the bottom, pluck the pods of okra when tender, and without bruising pack them on a layer of salt. Then follow with another layer of salt, following with another layer of okra, until the jar is full. Cover closely and put the jar in a cool place. There is another process, very simple, but not so good: Cut the okra into chips or shreds, dry them carefully, and pack away, so as not to be exposed to the air.—*Farmer and Planter*, April 1861

COOKING GREEN PEAS. Not one cook out of a hundred knows how to prepare the common "English" pea properly for the table. We have a method which renders them exceedingly nice: When shelled, put the peas in suffi-cient *boiling water* to cover them. When quite "done," put at the rate of one pint of milk to each quart of peas, and add, for the same quantity, one tablespoonful each of butter, sugar, and flour, and salt and pepper to taste. Boil all together five or ten minutes, and serve up.—*Southern Cultivator*, May–June 1862

FRIED POTATOES. How few cooks know how to fry potatoes. There is nothing so easy to get and yet so palatable for breakfast, with a thick, tender beef-steak, or a mutton chop fizzing from the grid-iron. To fry raw potatoes properly, they should be pared, cut lengthwise into slices an eighth of an inch in thickness, dropped into a pan over a fire containing hot beef drippings, turned frequently, nicely browned all over, but never burned. The addition of a little salt and pepper, while in the pan, and a little flour dredged over them, is an improvement. (So says some anonymous but sensible cook.) We have, however, found that a thick slice of good salt pork, instead of the "beef drip-pings," answered well. Everyone to his taste.—*Edgefield Advertiser*, March 19, 1863

WATERY POTATOES. We every day hear complaints about watery potatoes. Put into the pot a piece of lime as large as a hen's egg; and, how watery soever the potatoes may have been, when the water is poured off, the potatoes will be perfectly dry and mealy.—*Field and Fireside*, February 13, 1864

TO SAVE SWEET POTATOES. Always dig before frost and when the ground is very dry; have your beds ready by raising them about ten inches above the ground; then put on them dry straw about one foot deep; then put on the potatoes, about twenty-five bushels to a bank; next put straw one foot deep on them, dirt at least one foot thick, well packed. Shelter them with a good shelter to keep them dry. Leave no air hole, but rather try to exclude the air entirely. Potatoes thus put up are not affected by the changes of weather, which generally rot the potatoes. If dug when the ground is wet, they are almost certain to rot.—*Albany Patriot*, August 8, 1861

DRIED PUMPKINS. A distinguished physician requests the editor of the Vicksburg Whig to say there is nothing better for soldiers confined in camp

THE CONFEDERATE HOUSEWIFE

during the winter, when fruits and vegetables cannot be had, than dried pumpkins. He says that soaked in water until they are softened, and stewed with molasses, they are not only wholesome, but very palatable and an excellent substitute for fruits or vegetables. They can be cut into strips, hung up and dried, with great facility; then they can be packed in bags and sent to the army. They are now plenty and cheap in this section of the country.—*Edgefield Advertiser*, November 20, 1861

TO DRESS RICE. A lady recommends the following: Soak the rice in cold salt and water for seven hours. Have ready a stew pan with boiling water, throw in the rice, and let it boil briskly for ten minutes. Drain it in a colander, cover it up hot by the fire for a few minutes, then serve. The grains will be found double the usual size and quite distinct from each other.—*Field and Fireside*, January 10, 1863

DRIED TOMATOES. Take ripe tomatoes and scald them in the usual way. Strip off the skins and mash or squeeze them through a sieve. Then stew the pulp slowly, so as to evaporate as much as possible without burning. Spread on plates and dry in a slow oven or in the hot sun. When wanted to use, you have only to soak and cook a few minutes. Serve up as you would tomatoes stewed fresh from the garden.—*Field and Fireside*, June 6, 1863

BUT THEY ARE CORNFIELD PEAS STILL

May 4, 1865 — In spite of all we can do, there is a look of scantiness about the table that makes people afraid to eat as much as they want—and the dreadful things we have to give them, at that! Cornfield peas have been our stable diet for the last ten days. Mother has them cooked in every variety of style she ever heard of, but they are cornfield peas still. All this would have been horribly mortifying a year or two ago, but everybody knows how it is now, and I am glad to have even cornfield peas to share with our soldiers. Three cavalry officers ate dinner at the house while we were at Aunt Sallie's. Mother says they were evidently gentlemen, but they were so ragged and dirty that she thought the poor fellows did not like to give their names. They didn't introduce themselves, and she didn't ask who they were.

—**Andrews,** *War-Time Journal,* 209–10.

After considerable wandering, Eliza Andrews and her family were now in Washington, Ga.

JOHN HAMMOND MOORE

Meats & Fish

HOW TO SELECT POULTRY. A young turkey has a smooth dark leg, feet supple and moist, and the end of the breast bone pliable like gristle. If the head is on, the eyes will be full and bright if fresh killed. Fowls, when young, have smooth combs and legs. In other respects they are like young turkeys. Young geese will have yellow bills and feet, and a pin head may be forced through the skin of the breast. (It requires considerable pressure to thrust a pin through the breast of an old, tough goose.) If fresh, the feet will be pliable. The rules apply to the selection of ducks. As a general rule, all old birds have bony claws, that are not easily straightened. Young birds have pliant and easily yielding claws. The spurs of old turkeys and roosters are hard, long, and sharp. Of young ones, but the first development is seen.—*Southern Confederacy*, August 13, 1862

HOW TO FRY CHICKEN. Make a batter of two eggs, a teacup of milk, and a little salt, and thicken with flour; have the chickens cut up, washed, and seasoned; dip the pieces separately in the batter and fry them in hot lard. When brown on both sides, take them up and make a gravy. Lard fries much nicer than butter, which is apt to burn.

STEWED CHICKEN WITH RICE. The rice must first be soaked in water and very nicely washed, or it will not appear white. Two teacupfuls of rice are enough for one chicken, and must be boiled in a quart of water with a dessert spoonful of salt. The water should be boiling when the rice is put in, keep it boiling half an hour, then drain off the water, if the rice has not absorbed it, and place it in the bottom of the dish. The chicken must be in preparation at the same time as the rice, and should be cut up in joints, as for fried chicken, and salted and seasoned. Boil it in a little more water than sufficient to cover it, and when it is done, take it out and lay it over the rice on the dish. Then rub a small piece of butter with sufficient flour to thicken it, and stir both together in the liquor which must remain over the fire a few minutes; and, just before it is taken up, add the yolk of an egg well beaten and some chopped parsley. It must then be immediately poured over the chicken.—*Southern Cultivator*, April 1861

CHICKEN AND CORN PIE. Cut up two chickens, pepper and salt them. Grate six ears of green corn, to which add a pint of milk, three eggs, and a large spoonful of butter. Season with pepper and salt. Put some of this batter in a baking pan. Lay the chicken on it and then cover them with the rest of the batter. It will bake in about half an hour.—*Field and Fireside*, August 8, 1863

VIRGINIA STEW. Take two young chickens, cut them up, and parboil them; then peel and cook one quart of Irish potatoes; then peel and cut up one dozen large, ripe tomatoes; then cut the corn off one dozen soft roasting ears and mash it up; add to these one large onion, cut up fine. Put all in a stew pan and stew for two hours, stirring frequently to prevent burning. Extract the bones of the fowl; season with salt, butter, and pepper, and serve hot. If, after a fair trial, you pronounce this an unpalatable dish, then your loyalty to the Southern Confederacy ought to be questioned.—*Southern Recorder*, September 2, 1862

MOCK TERRAPIN. Boil the chicken until the meat is tender; then cut up in small pieces, say about the same size as we would a terrapin, removing all the large bones and rough parts, but especially retaining the wings and "drumsticks." Then put in a stew pot and dress precisely as for a terrapin, viz: butter, salt, cayenne pepper, cream, a little flour, the yolk of an egg well beaten, and some powdered sugar. Just before dishing, add one or two glasses of Maderia to suit the taste. This is a new dish, and when a "chicken fixen" is desired for company or otherwise, it is exceedingly handy and very "nice."   —*Southern Cultivator*, February 1861

TO BOIL A DUCK. Salt it two days. Boil half an hour, then fill with white bread, sage, onions, and butter rubbed together. Pepper and salt to taste. Return the duck to the pot and boil until done.—*Field and Fireside*, February 7, 1863

A RECIPE FOR PUTTING UP BEEF. A gentleman who has tried the following recipe warmly recommends it: Cut the beef into pieces of the proper size for packing, sprinkle them with salt lightly, and let them be twenty-four hours, after which shake off the salt and pack them in a barrel. In ten gallons of water, put four gallons salt, one pound saltpetre, half pound black pepper, half pound allspice, and half gallon of sugar. Place the mixture in a vessel over a slow fire and bring to a boil. Then take it off and, when it has cooled, pour it over the beef sufficient to cover it and fill the barrel. After the lapse of three or four days, turn the barrel upside down to be sure the beef is all covered by the brine. If the beef is good, it will make it fit to set before a king. The beef will keep for a good long time. During the scarcity and exorbitant price of bacon, our readers might try the recipe and test its virtues.—*Albany Patriot*, October 31, 1861

SALT BEEF. How the army cooks it may be useful at this time. Salt beef comes in pieces from eight to twelve pounds in weight. Before being cooked, they should be well washed and soaked in cold water for twenty-four hours, changing the water three times. For boiling, the beef should be placed in a stew pan of cold water, and made to boil quickly. As soon as the water boils, the meat must be taken out, the water thrown away, and fresh water placed in the pot, while the meat is still warm. Then boil it the usual time, according to the description of the joint. To bake or roast, prepare the meat as above, make a paste of flour and water, and bake in a slow oven for twenty minutes for each pound. Do not cut until cold.

For stewed salt beef, prepare it as above, and cut it into steaks of the usual thickness. Have some cabbage or other greens ready boiled, chop them up, and put in a stew pan with the meat, together with a gill of water to every pound of meat and one teaspoonful of pepper to every four pounds of meat. Stew gently for two hours. To vary the flavor, carrots, potatoes, haricot beans, boiled macaroni, cut up in pieces about an inch long, may be added.—*Yorkville Enquirer*, June 13, 1861

BROILED BEEF STEAK. It should be cut from a well-kept rump, and they are generally liked about three-quarters of an inch thick. Most cooks beat them with a rolling pin for ten minutes; but, if the meat is of good quality and the rump has been well kept, there will be no necessity for this. Just before finishing, rub a lump of butter over and lightly dredge with pepper and salt. Pickles and scraped horse-radish make a good garnish, and, for sauce, suit yourself.—*Southern Cultivator*, February 1861

CORNED BEEF—WITH WATER. For pickling one hundred pounds of beef, take six gallons of water, nine pounds of salt, three pounds of brown sugar, one quart of molasses, three ounces saltpetre, one ounce red pepper, and one ounce potash. Boil meat, skim well, and let stand until entirely cool. Then, having rubbed it with fine salt and packed it closely in a water-tight cask, pour the brine over it. After standing six weeks, re-boil the brine and return it to the tub. Or, if you prefer making it into bacon, take it out of the brine at the end of the six weeks and smoke well with hickory green wood. This recipe answers admirably for curing hams also.—*Field and Fireside*, October 26, 1861

CORNED BEEF—WITHOUT WATER. To every twenty-five pounds of beef put one ounce of saltpetre and one pound of brown sugar, although one quart of molasses will do as well. Rub the beef well with the mixture and place it in a barrel so the liquor exuded by the beef will cover it. Turn every day, and in a week you will have a fine corned beef. No water should be used. To preserve for a long time, after a week pour off the liquor, boil it a short time until the scum rises, remove that, and, when cold, pour it again over the beef. Beef so prepared will keep for many months and be equal to the best "Mess." For family use there is no better recipe. For plantation use a little more salt may be used. Beef so prepared may be kept for a long time without becoming hard.—*Field and Fireside*, December 14, 1861

RECIPE FOR BEEF HAMS. Cut out the entire bone of the hind quarter and rub in—every day, for a week—equal parts of salt and sugar. After this, hang them up to drip, in a cool, dry place for three days. Then take them down and, for every thirty pounds of beef, mix together one ounce of salt, one ounce ground pepper, and a half ounce of ground clove. Rub every part of the surface with the mixture thoroughly. The ham must now be rolled in a cylindrical form, swilling it round from the narrow to the thickest end, [then tie] with a stout cord or tape, and hang it up for ten days, when it will be ready for use. Hams made in this way are the finest in the world—a luxury.—*Field and Fireside*, March 15, 1862

TO RESTORE TAINTED MEAT. If your meat is tainted, take it out of the pickle. Wash so as to cleanse it of the offensive pickle. Then wash your barrel well with a solution either of lime or ashes, after which re-pack it, and between every layer of meat put a layer of charcoal until your barrel is full. Then make a fresh pickle strong enough to bear an egg and fill up your barrel. As you re-pack your pieces, it would be well to rub each piece with salt. Let it remain a week or ten days, and the taint will have disappeared, and the meat will be restored to its original sweetness.—*Field and Fireside*, January 17, 1863

VEAL CUTLETS. Cut good frying veal in slices near an inch thick; wash, drain, and season it; beat up an egg and have ready some pounded crackers and bread crumbs; dip the meat first in the beaten egg, and then in the bread, and fry it in hot lard. Mix a gravy of flour and water with salt and pepper. When the veal is taken up, pour it in and let it boil for a few minutes, then pour it over the veal. Grate a little nutmeg over it, if you choose.—*Southern Cultivator*, April 1861

MEAT BALLS. A savory way of preparing meat is in the form of meat balls thus made: Put cold boiled or raw beef or pork chopped very fine into a dish together with eggs—one to each half pound of meat. Add crumbs of light bread, soaked and mashed fine, and a couple of medium-sized chopped onions (may be omitted if not liked). Season to taste with salt, if meat is fresh, pepper, nutmeg, and allspice. Form into egg-shaped balls with the hand. If too moist to form well, add a little flour and fry in plenty of lard.—*Field and Fireside*, February 7, 1863

MOCK BRAWN. Boil a pair of neat's feet very tender, cut off the meat, and have ready a belly piece of pork salted with common salt and saltpetre for a week. Boil it almost enough, take out the bones, and roll the meat of the feet and pork together. Roll it very tight with a strong cloth and tie it with tape. Boil it till very tender and hang it up in the cloth till cold.—*Southern Confederacy*, March 12, 1861

BACON, ASHES AND SALT. During the Revolution, good bacon was made with a peck of salt and an abundance of hickory ashes to six hundred pounds. In applying the ashes, it is well to have a bucket of molasses, and apply a portion with a white-washing brush to each joint. When well smeared, rub on the ashes, which will thus adhere firmly and make an impenetrable cement. Let the experiment be tried. If the consumption of salt could thus be diminished, so as to disappoint the expectations of greedy speculators, it would be a public blessing.—*Charleston Mercury,* November 26, 1861

TO KEEP HAMS IN SUMMER. Cut in slices and trim off the rind and outside. Fry it about half as much as you would for the table. Pack tightly in jars. Pour over it the fat that fries out and enough lard to cover. Close the jar tightly, set in cool place, and it will keep fresh all summer.—*Field and Fireside,* March 7, 1863

TO KEEP MEAT FROM SPOILING IN SUMMER. Eat it early in the spring.—*Confederate States Almanac, 1865*

PRESERVING HAMS. Hang on the upper tier, smoke as long as you like, take them off, and lay on sticks with the flesh side up, and cover with perfectly dry, unbleached ashes, as much as you can put on. They must be above the rest of the meat, to prevent them being dripped on, as the taste of the ham might be injured by getting ashes wet by grease or rain. If the hogs are killed late in the season, it is not necessary to finish smoking before applying the ashes, as it can be just as well done after ashing as before. Two boys can ash one hundred hams in two or three hours.—*Southern Cultivator,* February 1861

TO PREVENT SKIPPERS IN HAM. There is nothing easier than to avoid the skippers and all other worms and bugs that usually infest and often destroy so much bacon. It is simply to keep your smokehouse dark, and the moth that deposits the egg will never enter it. For the past twenty-five years, I have attended to this, and never have had my bacon troubled by insects.—*Spartanburg Express,* February 19, 1862

A GOOD DISH. A lady of our acquaintance dropped in conversation the other day a recipe for garnishing fried ham; we walked off and wrote it down as well as we could remember the items. Our people have tried it and pronounce it an admirable help-out to the aforesaid ham. We print it for such as may choose to try it on: After the ham (or shoulder) is fried, take a portion of the grease out of the pan to use with the preparation about to be made; make gravy for the ham with the rest of the grease. Keep the first portion of the grease very hot, and pour into it a stiff batter made of corn meal, with a little flour, a little milk, a little butter, one egg, a few eschallots cut up very fine, salt, pepper, &c. Fry it brown on both sides. Then turn it into a dish, place your ham on it, and pour on the gravy,—and you have an excellent hard times dish. A few leaves of fresh lettuce scattered over the dish would not be amiss.—*Edgefield Advertiser,* March 4, 1863

BAKED HAM. Most people boil hams. It is much better when properly baked. Soak it for an hour in clean water and then wipe it dry. Next, spread it all over with thin butter, and then put it into a deep dish with sticks under it, to keep it out of the gravy. When it is fully done, take off the skin and matter crusted on the flesh side, and set it away to cool. You will find it very delicious, but too rich for dyspeptics. Try it, ye ham-eaters.—*Tri-Weekly Watchman*, June 5, 1861

TO STUFF HAM. Take a ham well smoked and washed (let the skin remain on) and make incisions all over the top two inches deep. Stuff them full of chopped parsley and some pepper. To be eaten cold.—*Field and Fireside*, January 17, 1863

HAM TOAST. Boil a quarter of a pound of lean ham, chop it small, and mix with the yolks of three eggs well beaten, half an ounce of butter, two tablespoons of cream, and a little cayenne. Stir it over a fire till it thickens and spread it on hot toast with the crust cut off. Garnish with parsley.—*Farmer and Planter*, June 1861

NONPAREIL SAUCE. Take a slice of boiled ham, as much breast of roasted fowl, a pickled cucumber, a yolk of a hard-boiled egg, one anchovy, a little parsley, and a head of a shallot chopped very fine. Boil a moment in good catsup and use for meat or fish.—*Field and Fireside*, January 25, 1863

FOR SAUSAGE. Take one or two pounds of brown sugar to one hundred pounds of meat, mix with pepper and salt, and let no water come in contact with the meat. The sugar prevents the sausage from becoming strong.—*Spartanburg Express*, December 18, 1861

SAUSAGE MEAT. After several years experience, I have found the following recipe to be the best for preparing sausage meat I have ever seen. To fifty pounds of chopped meat, add one and one-fourth pounds of salt, four ounces of good black pepper, and fourteen tablespoonfuls of sage.—*Clarke's Confederate Household Almanac*, 1863

SAUSAGES. Sausages can be made by using mutton instead of pork. Chop lean and fat mutton together very fine and season with sage, salt, and pepper. Eat with mustard, and they cannot be distinguished from the genuine pork sausage.—*Field and Fireside*, March 14, 1863

TO CLEAN A PIG'S HEAD. Chop off the snout from the head and divide it into four pieces, after cutting off the cheeks to salt, saving them to bake with beans. Wash all thoroughly, put in a suitable vessel, and cover with water in which a little salt has been added to draw off the blood. Let soak two days, changing the water each day. The third day, take from the water and scrape well, but without attempting to remove the bristle. If bristles do not seem pretty dry after scraping, wipe the skin side. Then light a spirit lamp and singe off the bristles. It will take them off completely, leaving the pieces white and smooth after a slight scraping.—*Field and Fireside,* May 16, 1863

I Do Wish You Were Here to Eat the Brains

I am in the middle of Hog killing, and can only catch time to write a few lines. We killed 14 of the <u>best</u> ones yesterday and they only weighed 2021 pounds, small meat it is, but the Hogs are none of them more than 18 months old, we have 10 more to kill which I hope will make 1000 pounds more— This is a small allowance but with the Beef, and molasses we can make out with it. I do wish so much that you were here to eat the Brains, and Sausages. I shall try to save you some any how still hoping you will get home at Christmas or New Years.

—Jane McLure of Pacolet Mills, S.C., to her husband in Virginia, December 14, 1864, McLure Family Papers

"POW HAUS"—A DUTCH BREAKFAST DISH. Take a pig's head and feet, boil them until the meat falls from the bones, and then withdraw them from the liquor they were boiled in, which strain and return to the pot. Chop up the meat very fine, season it with pepper, salt, spice, and onions, chopped fine, thyme, sage, parsley, &c., and put it into the liquor, adding a sufficient quantity of corn meal to make a stiff mush. Set the pot on and let it boil *ten* minutes, stirring it well the whole time. Then pour it into a deep pan and, when cold, cut it into thin slices and fry it—and serve it to the table hot. The skin and bones, left from making sausages, will answer equally well; made the same way.—*Southern Cultivator,* January–February 1863

HINTS ON COOKING MUTTON
ROASTING. The hind quarter is best for roasting, but the leg, loin, neck, and breast are also good. The process of cooking is similar to that of

THE CONFEDERATE HOUSEWIFE

beef, about twenty minutes per pound. Baste with salt and water till nearly done, then add flour to the basting and let it brown. Put paper over the fat parts.

BOILING. The leg is good for boiling. Boil the same as beef. A large piece, say ten pounds, will require three hours boiling. Save the shank-bone for soup.

MUTTON BROTH. Take the liquor in which the leg was boiled, put in the shank, while it is cold. When done, thicken with rice and (if liked) season with parsley.

STUFFED LOIN OF MUTTON. Take off the skin, bone it neatly, and stuff the inside where the bones have been removed. Roll it up tight, skewer the flap and tie it down with twine. Put the outside skin over it until nearly done, and then remove it so that the mutton may brown. Serve with currant jelly, if you have it.

MUTTON CHOPS. Cut them from the loin or the best end of the neck. Dip them in beaten eggs, strew over them grated bread seasoned with salt, and fry on a soap-stone griddle, or better, broil them over coals.

LAMB AND VEAL. These meats require treatment similar to mutton and beef, but do not take as much cooking. Two hours will roast a fore-quarter of lamb.—*Southern Cultivator*, April 1861

CURRIE FOR RABBITS. Cut four middling-sized onions and two apples in slices and put them in a stew pan with two ounces of butter. Place over a moderate fire, stirring occasionally, until the onions are slightly brown and pulpy, when add two tablespoonfuls of currie powder and one of currie paste. Mix well, moisten with half a pint of stock or water, and let boil. Have a couple of young rabbits cut in joints and fried in butter in a frying pan to a

---

DINNER IN THE SHENANDOAH VALLEY, NOV. 1862

I spent one day and night with General Gregg, seeing General A. P. Hill, the Haskells . . . and other officers, and also many privates of my acquaintance from South Carolina, and dining with a Lexington company on a choice leg of mutton, nice biscuits and a cup of buttermilk. Next morning the owner of the land occupied by the camp reported to General Gregg that two of his best Merino sheep were missing, and I then suspected from what quarter my dinner of mutton had come, but said nothing.

—**Scott**, *Random Recollections*, 172

JOHN HAMMOND MOORE

nice brown color. Put into the currie sauce, season with a little [salt?] and juice of a lemon. Let stew gently over a very slow fire, stirring occasionally, until the rabbit is quite tender, when dress upon your dish and serve with rice, plain boiled, separate.—*Southern Confederacy*, March 12, 1861

FOR ENSURING THE SWEETNESS OF FISH CONVEYED BY LAND CARRIAGE TO ANY DISTANCE. The belly of the fish should be opened and the internal parts sprinkled with powdered charcoal. The same material will restore even putrescent fish to perfect freshness. Also, while on the subject, it may be well to add that charcoal, well pulverized, is the best tooth powder that can be used, both to keep the teeth white and to prevent their decay. To pulverize charcoal, heat it red hot on a shovel and then put it in a bottle of pure water. If you use the water with a tooth brush, it is still better.—*Field and Fireside*, August 8, 1863

SALTED FISH. A glass of vinegar put into the water you lay your fish in to soak will fetch out most of the salt.—*Field and Fireside*, January 10, 1863

TO PRESERVE FISH

With oil: Put the fish in jars and pour over them salad oil until they are covered, then tie them up air-tight. This is a rather expensive method in this country, but for fish that is afterwards fried, it is excellent.

With acid: Dip them into or brush over them pyroligenous acid and then dry them by exposure to the air. This gives a smoky flavor, but if strong vinegar or pure acetic acid be used, no taste will be imparted. It may be applied by means of a painter's clean brush, or even a stiff feather. A tablespoonful is enough to brush over a large surface. Fish and flesh so prepared will bear a voyage to the East Indies and back.

With sugar: Fish may be preserved in a dry state, and kept quite fresh by means of sugar alone, and even with a small quantity of it. Fish may be kept in that state for some days, so as to be as good when boiled as if just caught. If dried, and free from mouldiness, there seems no limit to their preservation, and they are much better in this way than when salted. The sugar has no disagreeable taste. The process is particularly valuable in making what is called kippered salmon, and the fish preserved in this manner are far superior in quality and flavor to those which are salted or smoked. If desired, as much salt may be used to give the taste that may be required.—*Southern Cultivator*, March–April 1863

TO BOIL STURGEON. Having cleaned the sturgeon well, boil the desired quantity to as much water as will just cover it, with two or three bits of lemon peel, some whole peppers, a stick of horse-radish, and a pint of vinegar to every half gallon of water. When done, garnish with fried oysters, sliced lemon, and horse-radish. Serve with melted butter or anchovy sauce.—*Field and Fireside*, February 7, 1863

STURGEON MEAT AND OIL. The *Raleigh Standard* calls attention to the importance of saving for use the sturgeons now abounding in our large rivers. Parboil the meat until the oil is out; then put it on slats to drip; as soon as cool, sprinkle salt on it, a half bushel to one thousand pounds; after remaining in salt one day, hang up and smoke. In order to obtain the oil, take the head and skin, cut in small pieces, and boil as long as any oil rises to the surface. Put this with the skimmings of the meat and boil gently until the sediment has settled. The meat, thus cured is said to be good, and the oil is useful for lamps and machinery.—*Southern Cultivator*, September–October 1863

SCALLOPED OYSTERS. Wash your oysters well in their own liquor. Then put some of them into scallop shells or a deep dish, strew over them a few bread crumbs, with some seasoning, such as you prefer, and spread some butter on them. Then add another layer of oysters, then of bread crumbs, &c., and when the dish or shells are full enough, spread some butter over the top and put them in an oven to brown.

PICKLED OYSTERS. Boil the oysters in their own liquor until they look plump, then take them out and strain the liquor. Add to it wine, vinegar, and pepper to your taste, and pour it over the oysters.—*Farmer and Planter*, March 1861

TO STEW TERRAPINS. Plunge them in boiling water till they are dead. Take them out, pull off the outer skins and toenails, and wash in warm water. Then boil with a teaspoon of salt for each middling-sized terrapin till you can pinch the flesh off the bone of the leg. Turn them out of the shell into a dish, remove the sand bags and gall, and add the yolks of three eggs. Cut up your meat and season high with equal parts of black and cayenne pepper and salt. Put all in a sauce pan with the liquor they have given out in cutting up, but not a drop of water. Add a quarter pound of butter with a gill of Madeira to every two terrapins. Simmer gently till tender, closely covered. Thicken with flour and serve hot.—*Field and Fireside*, April 5, 1862

Vinegar, Pickles, &c.

TO MAKE VINEGAR. Fill large glass bottles with weak tea, which may be what is left over after drinking. Add a small quantity of sugar or molasses and set in a warm place, say in a window where the sun shines. In a fortnight, it will be fit for use and is as good as cider vinegar.—*Edgefield Advertiser*, February 7, 1863

CIDER VINEGAR. Take six quarts of corn meal, stir and mix well into a barrel of strong cider of the best kind, and then add a gallon of whiskey. Cover the cask (leaving the bung loosely in it) and set in the part of your yard most exposed to the sun and air. In the course of four weeks, if the weather is warm and dry, you will have a good vinegar fit for use. When you draw off a gallon or more, replenish the cask with the same quantity of cider and add about a pint of whiskey. You may thus have a vinegar constantly at hand for common purposes. The cask should have iron hoops.

HONEY VINEGAR #1. A strong vinegar may be made by mixing cider and strained honey, allowing a pound of honey to a gallon of cider, and letting it stand for five or six months. This vinegar is so powerful that for common purposes it should be diluted with a little water.

HONEY VINEGAR #2. To one quart of clear honey, put eight quarts of warm water and mix well. When it has passed through the acetous fermentation, a white vinegar will be formed, in many respects better than the ordinary vinegar.

SUGAR VINEGAR. To one measure of sugar, put seven measures of water moderately warm. Dissolve it completely and put into a cask, mixing in yeast in proportion of a pint to eight gallons of water. Stop it close and keep in a warm place until sufficiently sour.—*Field and Fireside*, June 13, 1863

WHITE VINEGAR. Put in a cask a mixture composed of five gallons of water, two gallons of whiskey, and a quart of yeast, stirring in two pounds of powdered charcoal. Place it where it will ferment properly, leaving the bung loose until the fermentation is over, but covering the hole slightly to keep out the dust and insects. At the end of four months, draw it off, and you will have a fine vinegar as clear and colorless as water.—*Field and Fireside*, May 30, 1863

SPICED VINEGAR. For every pint of spiced vinegar it is intended to make, take one ounce of black pepper, half an ounce of salt, half an ounce of ginger, a quarter of an ounce of allspice, and, if desired to be hot, add also a quarter of a drachm of cayenne or a few capsicums. Bruise the whole of these materials in a mortar, and put them in a jar, or wide-mouthed, green glass bottle, tied over with a bladder. Place this in a saucepan of water and keep it hot for three days, shaking it now and then. If the maker has an enamel saucepan, this operation can be facilitated by simmering the ingredients together. Spiced vinegar is used hot for walnuts and cool for cabbages.—*Carolina Spartan*, April 17, 1862

PEPPER VINEGAR. Get one dozen pods of pepper when ripe, take out the stems, and cut them in two. Put them in a kettle with three pints of vinegar, boil away one quart, and strain through a sieve. A little of this is excellent in gravy of every kind and gives a flavor greatly superior to black pepper. It is always very fine when added to each of the various catsups for fish sauce.—*Edgefield Advertiser*, August 28, 1861

GRAPE VINEGAR. Put the pulp and skins, after pressing the grapes to make wine, also the half ripe and partially decayed grapes, in a good whiskey barrel. To every gallon of juice, pressed out, add a gallon of water to the pulp, and a half gallon of molasses to every gallon of water. Tie an old blanket or piece of homespun over the head of the barrel. When the skins, &c., rise to the top, press them down. As soon as it becomes sharp, the liquid should be drawn off into demijohns. It is usually ready in ten to fifteen days, and will be fit for use a few days after drawn off, if properly made.—*Field and Fireside*, December 7, 1861

SALAD DRESSING. One cup of good cider, a teaspoon of oil, one of made mustard, a salt-spoon of salt, and the yolk of a hard-boiled egg rubbed fine. Pour over the salad and send to the table.—*Field and Fireside*, January 17, 1863

SUBSTITUTES FOR BLACK PEPPER AND MUSTARD. An esteemed correspondent of Gainesville, Ala., writes us: "I will give you a receipt for making black pepper, and I could not tell the difference from the genuine. Prepare some red pepper tea, as strong as long boiling will make it. Soak fine wheat in it till saturated, then parch the wheat brown outside, and grind it. To take the place of mustard—take the inside of walnut bark, heat it up and make a plaster, and it will draw and even blister."—*Southern Banner*, March 15, 1865

VALUABLE PICKLING RECIPES: GOOD FOR PICKLING PEACHES OR PEARS. Pare the fruit, then add one-half pound of sugar to every pound of fruit. Put them in a jar, a layer of fruit and then a sprinkling of sugar, and let them stand over night. To the juice thus expressed, add vinegar enough to cover them, cook a short time, and they are done. Spice as you please. I learned from a German lady (an excellent housekeeper) that a piece of horse-radish root put into the jar with any kind of pickles, will prevent scum from rising. We need only to try it to prove it.

WATERMELON PICKLES. Ten pounds of watermelon rinds boiled in pure water until they are tender. Drain the water off, then make a syrup of two pounds of sugar, one quart of vinegar, half an ounce of cloves, and one ounce of cinnamon. The syrup is to be boiled and poured over the rinds boiling hot. Drain the syrup off and let it come to a boil, pour it over the melon three times in succession. The rind prepared in this way far surpasses any pickle I ever have eaten. It will keep this way from one year to another.

TOMATO AND ONION PICKLES. To one quart of vinegar, add half a pound of brown sugar, half an ounce of cloves, and one ounce of cinnamon buds. Select small onions, boil in the vinegar three minutes, skim them out; when cool, lay them down in a crock—first a layer of onions, and then tomatoes (the small plum tomato is the best), and when the vinegar is cold, pour it over them and set in a cool place.—*Tri-Weekly Watchman*, August 12, 1861

PICKLED TOMATOES. Gather the small red tomatoes, with stems on, as soon as ripe—not too ripe—early in the morning. They must be quite fresh when prepared. Wash in cold water and drain thoroughly. Then put them into a jar with the stems downward, a layer of tomatoes and a layer of brown sugar alternately. Boil a sufficient quantity of vinegar to cover them, putting in spices to season. Let the vinegar stand till cold, then pour it over the tomatoes. Prepared in this way, they will be ready for use in two weeks and will keep through the winter.—*Field and Fireside*, July 11, 1863

GREEN TOMATO PICKLES. Take tomatoes after they have grown to their full size and slice them thin. Scald them an instant in salted water, and then lay them in a jar with vinegar, cloves, and cinnamon.—*Spartanburg Express*, August 14, 1861

TO PICKLE FIGS. When the figs are fully grown and about to soften, but still firm, gather them, put in jars, and pour on hot, unspiced vinegar enough to cover. Let them remain a few days, then pour off the vinegar, which will be found to be exceedingly sweet, unpleasantly so. To this a little water may be added, and it goes to increase the contents of the vinegar barrel; or, if the vinegar is weak, pour it in as it is without water, and it will soon improve in strength. The pickles then should be put in suitable jars and covered with good sharp vinegar spiced to the taste, poured on hot, and the jars corked and closed with wax. It is better not to add salt to the jars until opened for use, but the other spices should be added before sealing up.—*Edgefield Advertiser*, July 23, 1863

AXE JAR PICKLES (delicious). Take one gallon of best white vinegar, two dozen nutmegs, two ounces of mace, one pound of green ginger, one pound of allspice, two ounces of cloves, three ounces of tumeric, one pound of English mustard seed, half a pound of eschalots (or shallots), one vial of flour of mustard, and half a pound of garlic, which must be put on small sticks. The vegetables for pickling must be covered with salt three days, then taken out and dried in the sun the same length of time. Their shrivelled appearance must not discourage the housekeeper: they become plump and full when kept for some time in the vinegar, which must not be boiled, as in most pickles. They also improve with age.—*Due-West Telescope*, September 20, 1861

SWEET CHERRY PICKLES. By Mrs. Dr. E. Sill of Columbia. To three pounds of cherries, add one pound of refined sugar, in powder. To these add half an ounce of cinnamon, half an ounce of mace, bruised, and fill a two-gallon jar with cold vinegar.—*Farmer and Planter*, June 1861

CABBAGE PICKLES. Put a plate of onions to an ordinary-sized kettle of cabbage, one tumbler of white sugar, or more if you wish them sweet, one tumbler of mustard seed, two spoonfuls of mustard, two of salt, and two of black pepper. Add allspice and other spices, if you like, and a small piece of alum—cover the whole with vinegar and boil rapidly until the cabbage is cooked.—*Field and Fireside*, June 15, 1861

RECIPE FOR TOMATO CATSUP. Extra good, by a lady of Griffin, Georgia. Mix one-half bushel of ripe tomatoes, three boxes of mustard, three pounds of brown sugar, one pound of salt, one quart of vinegar, one-fourth pound each of black pepper, allspice, and cloves, six large onions, a handful of peach leaves, and two ounces of cayenne pepper (common red will answer). Simmer the whole three hours, then strain through a wire sieve or coarse muslin. Bottle and seal closely, and keep, as age improves the catsup.—*Southern Confederacy*, August 23, 1862

GREEN TOMATO CATSUP THAT WILL KEEP BOTH SUMMER AND WINTER. Pick a bushel of tomatoes when quite green, cut off the stems, boil soft, rub through a sieve, set the pulp on the fire, and season highly with red pepper; of cloves, allspice, and mace, each half an ounce; salt to taste. To this add a half gallon of good vinegar and boil half an hour. If liked, add four onions, chopped fine. Will keep without sealing.—*Southern Recorder*, March 29, 1864

RED PEPPER CATSUP. As our patriotic ladies are preparing many good and useful things for the soldiers, many of whom have been sick and need something to give them appetite and strength, allow me through your valuable journal, to offer them a recipe for making red pepper catsup. I have used it in my family and think it is the best article for flavoring soups and fresh meats that I have ever used. Take four dozen pepper pods (ripe or green), two quarts of vinegar, one quart of water, three tablespoonfuls of grated horse-radish, five onions, and one handful of garlic. Boil until soft, then strain through a sieve and add two tablespoonfuls of black pepper, two tablespoonfuls of salt, one each of spice and mace, and half a tablespoonful of cloves. Then boil ten minutes, bottle, and seal for use. Mary L. Purifoy, Mount Meigs.—*Southern Recorder,* October 22, 1861

WALNUT CATSUP. Take one hundred walnuts, beat them up fine, add one gallon of vinegar, boil together, and strain off. Then add one tablespoonful each of salt, pepper, cloves, allspice, cinnamon, and mace, and two nutmegs. Boil all together, let cool, and bottle for use.—*Edgefield Advertiser,* June 19, 1861

CUCUMBER KETCHUP. Take three dozen full-grown cucumbers, chop them as fine as possible, and mix with several chopped onions. Sprinkle on three-quarters of a pint of fine table salt and put the whole in a sieve. Let drain twelve hours. Then add a teacupful of ground black pepper. Put the whole in a jar with the strongest vinegar. Close it up tightly for three days and it is fit for use. It will keep for years.—*Field and Fireside,* June 13, 1863

IMITATION OF WORCESTER SAUCE. Take one gallon ripe tomatoes, wash, and simmer them in three quarts of water. Boil it half down and strain through a sieve. When all is drained, add two tablespoonfuls of ginger, two of mace, two of whole pepper, two of salt, one of cloves, and one of cayenne. Let them simmer in juice until reduced to one quart. Pour in half a pint of best vinegar, then pour the whole through a hair sieve. Bottle in half-pint bottles, cork down tightly, seal, and keep in a cool place.—*Farmer and Planter,* August 1861

THE CONFEDERATE HOUSEWIFE

Puddings, Cakes & Pies

MRS. MANN'S RICE PUDDING. Swell a cupful of rice in milk or water (milk is preferable), add to it, when swelled, a quart of milk, five eggs, two teaspoonfuls of brown sugar, a little mace or cinnamon, a teaspoonful of salt, and a cupful of rich cream. Bake an hour and a half. Raisins may be added if desired. (This makes a rich pudding. We would consider it rather more wholesome with the eggs omitted.)

WHORTLEBERRY PUDDING. Take one pint of milk, three eggs, and flour enough for a stiff batter. When these are well mixed, add three pints of berries, tie the whole pretty tightly in a floured cloth, and boil two hours and a half. Serve with cream sauce.—*Southern Cultivator*, August 1861

CONFEDERATE PUDDING. One quart of milk, a pint of flour, eight eggs, a little salt, and one quart of dried apples cut up very small and well washed. Beat the eggs. Roll fruit in the flour and mix with milk and eggs. Flour a cloth well, pour in the pudding, tie up, and boil five or six hours. Eaten with butter and sugar sauce.—*Field and Fireside*, August 15, 1863

TO MAKE A CONFEDERATE PUDDING. Half a pound of raisins, half a pound of currants, half ounce of suet chopped fine, a pint of syrup, one pint of water, two eggs, a teaspoonful of saleratus, and add citron if you like. Mix with enough flour to make it the consistency of cake batter and boil two hours and a half. For the sauce, take a lump of grated nutmeg and a half pint of water. Boil all and thicken with flour. Add brandy to your taste, but don't get drunk.—*Carolina Spartan*, April 17, 1862

BAKED INDIAN PUDDING. Take one quart of corn meal, two quarts of warm milk (about blood heat), two tablespoonfuls of sugar, one teaspoonful of chopped suet, and half a grated nutmeg. Bake the mixture in a pan two hours.—*Field and Fireside*, February 14, 1863

BAKED GEORGIA PUDDING. Six eggs, two cups of sugar, three cups of flour, one cup of butter, one teaspoonful soda, and two teaspoonfuls cream of tartar dissolved in a cup of milk. Wash and cream the butter, add sugar, then the yellows of the eggs after they have been well beaten. Add a portion of dissolved cream of tartar to the butter, then the whites of the eggs, and finally the balance of the milk. Beat now very well, stir in flour lightly, and bake quickly—not more than twenty minutes.

BOILED GEORGIA PUDDING. Mix one-half pound of butter, three-fourths of a pound of sugar, one pound of flour, eight eggs, one-half teaspoonful of soda, one-half teaspoonful of cream of tartar, and one pound of raisins. Boil from two to three hours and serve hot with liquid or cold sauce. The raisins may be omitted.—*Field and Fireside*, February 7, 1863

TO MAKE HASTY PUDDING. Take a half dozen eggs, two tablespoonfuls of sugar, one cup of flour, a lump of butter large as an egg, and half a nutmeg. You may add, if you like, one-half pound of raisins. Mix well and bake quick.—*Farmer and Planter*, June 1861

TRANSPARENT PUDDING. Take the yolks of twelve eggs, beat to a froth, add sugar to make a stiff batter and a small bit of butter. Flavor with anything to suit your fancy. Have two good-sized pie plates lined with pastry. Pour the batter in and bake until done. Some pour preserves (small fruit) in the pastry before the batter.—*Field and Fireside*, June 27, 1863

IRISH POTATO PUDDING. One pound of butter, one pound of sugar, beat to a cream. One pound of potatoes boiled and passed through the colander, eight eggs well beaten, one glass of brandy, one of wine, half a glass of rose water, and one teaspoon of spice. Mix and cook as usual.—*McLeod Journal*

A BIRD'S NEST PUDDING. Pare and slice enough easily cooked apples to nearly fill a deep dish or basin. Make a batter of some cream, soda, and flour, with a little salt. Add to the apples a little water and some sugar. Pour the batter over and bake half an hour. Eat with sweetened cream and nutmeg.—*Farmer and Planter*, March 1861

A SIMPLE PUDDING. Boil a quart of milk. Cut up some bread in small pieces and soak them in the milk for about half an hour. Add a tablespoonful of Indian meal and a piece of butter the size of a walnut. Sweeten well and put in nutmeg and some other spices. Bake about twenty minutes.—*Field and Fireside*, January 17, 1863

TREACLE PUDDING. Take three tablespoonfuls of treacle, one of flour, and a little ground ginger. Mix all together. Line a basin or pan with paste. Spread some of the mixture in with a spoon. Then put a layer of paste, with the mixture spread over it, and so on until the basin or pan is full. Either baked or boiled, this pudding is said to be very good.

SNOW BALLS. Swell half a pound of rice in water with a roll of lemon peel until tender. Drain and divide into five parts. Roll a pared apple (cored and the hole filled with sugar and cinnamon) into each heap and tie each one tightly in separate cloths. Boil for an hour and serve with pudding sauce.—*Field and Fireside*, January 2, 1864

SWEET APPLE PUDDING. Take one pint of scalding milk, half a pint of Indian meal, a teaspoonful of salt, and six sweet apples cut in pieces. Bake hot less than three hours. The apples will afford an excellent rich jelly. This is truly one of the most luxurious yet simple puddings made.—*Field and Fireside*, February 13, 1864

THE CONFEDERATE HOUSEWIFE

PORCUPINE PUDDING. Take a flat sponge cake, stick blanched almonds all over it, and pour over it a rich custard, not to cover the almonds.—*Due-West Telescope*, September 20, 1861

CONFEDERATE SOLDIER'S PUDDING. To one quart of mush, add one teaspoonful of butter and stir in sufficient molasses to sweeten it. Beat up four large eggs, into which grate half a large nutmeg and one small teaspoonful of ginger. Flavor with essence of lemon. Mix all together. Have a large pudding pan or pie dish well greased with lard or butter, put in half of the pudding, then drop in preserves of any kind or stewed fruit. Put in the remaining part and bake one hour.—*Southern Enterprise*, September 11, 1861

SAUCES FOR PUDDINGS

CREAM SAUCE. Into half a pint of cream beat a cup of finely powdered sugar and flavor with a little lemon juice.

FRUIT SAUCE. Stew a dozen plums or cherries; boil a pint of cream and pour over it a pound of powdered sugar; add the fruit to the sugar and cream mixture, and flavor with lemon or rose water.

SUGAR SAUCE. Boil a pint of sifted brown sugar and add a cupful of sweet cream.

APPLE CREAM. Beat up six baked apples (having taken off the skins *after* baking) with the yolk of an egg and a tablespoonful of cream; then beat up the white of an egg separately and pour upon the top.—*Southern Cultivator*, August 1861

A SUBSTITUTE FOR CREAM SAUCE. Beat two eggs, mix well with one small teaspoonful of corn starch—stir into this one pint of boiling water—boil a few minutes—flavor with a few drops of lemon and sweeten to your taste.—*Southern Cultivator*, April 1861

GENERAL DIRECTIONS FOR CAKE MAKING. Have flour and sugar warm and devoid of lumps. Beat the whites and yolks of eggs separately. Wash currants in a hair sieve, rub well in a coarse table-cloth, dry in a heated room, and dust them with flour before using. Remove the stems and seeds from raisins, chop them, and dust with flour. Cut citron into small pieces, use ground spices, butter pan well, and place a white paper over it. If the top of the oven is hotter than the bottom, your cake will be heavy. Open the oven door no oftener than is necessary to turn the pan around. Dissolve subcarbonate of soda in hot water and mix cream of tartar thoroughly through the flour. Beat cake with a wooden spoon or spade. Melt butter by putting it in an earthen bowl and standing in a vessel of hot water. Never mix sour and sweet milk by dissolving soda in it. When your cake is nicely brown, pierce it in the middle with a broom splint and, if nothing adheres, it is done. A tin box or can is preferable to wooden ones for keeping cakes.—*Southern Federal Union*, June 18, 1861

WORTH KNOWING. A bowl containing two quarts of water, set in an oven while baking, will prevent pies, cakes, etc., from being scorched.—*Field and Fireside*, April 25, 1863

ELIZABETH CAKE. Mix one cup of butter, three cups of white sugar, four cups of flour, one cup of milk, four eggs (whites beaten to a froth), two tablespoonfuls of cream of tartar, and one teaspoonful of soda. Flavor with lemon and bake as usual.—*Due-West Telescope*, September 20, 1861

BATH CAKES. Mix well together a quarter of a pound of butter, half a pound of flour, two large eggs, and a tablespoonful of yeast. Set the mixture before the fire to rise, and when it has been affected, add two ounces of finely powdered sugar and half an ounce of caraways. Roll the paste out into little cakes; bake them on tins.—*Southern Confederacy*, March 12, 1861

CHRISTMAS CAKE, 1864

As the war continued everything went higher and higher. There was lots of money, but you could not get anything for it. Flour was five hundred dollars a barrel, and was hard to get at that. On Christmas, 1864, my mother sent me down town to get some sugar to make a cake. I got one pound of brown sugar and paid six dollars for it, and was glad to get it at that. Most of the cake consisted of corn meal and sorghum, and it was first-rate, too.

—Williams, *Columbia, 119–20*

CHEAP CAKE. Mix one tablespoonful of butter, one egg, one cup of sugar, one-half cup of buttermilk, one-half teaspoonful of soda, and flour enough to make a stiff batter. Flavor with lemon.—*Field and Fireside*, December 7, 1861

RAILROAD CAKE. Take one cup of flour, one cup of sugar, four table-spoonfuls of sweet milk, one tablespoonful of butter, two eggs, one teaspoonful of cream of tartar, and half a teaspoonful of soda. Beat ten minutes, then put in a pan and bake as usual.—*Farmer and Planter*, February 1861

JENNY LIND CAKE. Beat well together one coffee cup of butter and one pound of pulverized sugar. Add the yolks of six eggs and one cup of milk. Mix thoroughly. To four cups of flour add two teaspoonfuls of cream of tartar and sift gently over the mixture, stirring all the time. Add one teaspoonful of soda dissolved in one tablespoonful of warm water. Mix well. Stir in gently the whites of six eggs beaten to a stiff foam. You may flavor with lemon. Bake slowly. It should be put in the oven as soon as possible after putting in the soda and whites of eggs.—*Field and Fireside*, December 14, 1861

GINGER POUND CAKE. Cut up in a pan three-fourths pound of butter and a teacup of brown sugar. Mix with a pint of West Indian molasses and stir well together. Sift into a pan a pound of flour. In another, beat five eggs. Add gradually the eggs and flour to the mixture of butter, sugar, and molasses, together with two large tablespoonfuls of ground ginger and four of ground cinnamon. Then stir in a glass of brandy and a small teaspoonful of saleratus melted in a very little milk. Add a pound of raisins dredged with flour and transfer to a buttered tin pan, and bake from two to three hours.—*Field and Fireside*, April 11, 1863

CHEAP SPONGE CAKE. Two eggs, one cup of flour, one cup of sugar, one spoonful of sweet milk, half a spoonful of soda, one teaspoonful of cream of tartar, and a little salt. Grate in some rind of lemon and add a part of the juice and a teaspoonful of butter. Bake fifteen minutes.—*Field and Fireside*, March 7, 1863

COMMON CAKE. One cup of sugar, two of cream, one tablespoonful of saleratus, three eggs, and flour to make stiff.—*Field and Fireside*, June 6, 1863

MEASURE CAKE. Stir in a teacup of cream, a teacup of butter, and two of sugar. Then stir in four eggs beaten to a froth, a grated nutmeg, and a pint of flour. Stir until just before it is baked. It is good baked either in cups or pans.—*Field and Fireside*, October 5, 1861

RICE CAKE. A quarter of a pound of ground rice, a quarter of a pound of flour, half a pound of finely powdered white sugar, and five eggs. Beat all well together till it froth; pour quickly into a tin lined with buttered paper; bake three-quarters of an hour in a moderate oven. This does nicely for a tea cake. It may be flavored with almond and lemon.—*Field and Fireside*, May 16, 1863

Mr. Editors: In one of your papers a short time ago, you requested some of your subscribers to send you, if possible, some receipts which would be practicable in the now limited state of our larders. I send you a few which I have tried and have found them very good.

CONFEDERATE CAKE. One half pint of corn meal, one quart of stewed apples or peaches, three eggs, three large spoonfuls of sugar, a teaspoonful of lard, and another of yeast powder or a small spoon of soda. Mix, season with spice, cloves, and nutmeg, and bake in a slow oven.

GINGER CAKE. Four cups of flour, a dessert spoon of lard, a cup of molasses, a tablespoon of ginger, a cup of sugar, a teaspoon of soda, and three eggs. The soda must be dissolved in a tumbler of water. Mix and bake in small pans.

SIMPLE CAKE. Take two cups of wheat flour, one cup of milk, another of sugar, an egg, one teaspoonful of soda, and two teaspoonfuls of cream of tartar. Mix the latter with the dry flour. The soda must be dissolved in the milk and added first before baking.—*Field and Fireside*, August 15, 1863

PLAIN GINGERBREAD. Mix three pounds of flour with four ounces of moist sugar, half an ounce of powdered ginger, and one pound and a quarter of warm treacle. Melt half a pound of fresh butter in it, put it to the flour, and make a paste. Then form it into nuts or cakes, or bake it as one cake.

ANOTHER METHOD. Mix six pounds of flour with two ounces of caraway seeds, two ounces of ground ginger, two ounces of candied orange peel, the same of candied lemon peel cut into pieces, a little salt, and six ounces of moist sugar. Melt one pound of fresh butter into about half a pint of milk, pour it by degrees into four pounds of treacle, stir it well together, and add it, a little at a time, to the flour. Mix it thoroughly, make it into a paste, roll out rather thin, and cut into cakes with the top of a dredger or a wine glass. Put them on floured tins and bake them in a rather brisk oven.—*Field and Fireside*, October 26, 1861

CRISP GINGERBREAD. Take two cups of butter, two cups of molasses, a cup of sugar, a teaspoonful of soda dissolved in four tablespoonfuls of milk, and two tablespoonfuls of ginger. Add flour to make it stiff enough to roll out. Then roll out very thin on buttered tin sheets. Mark into squares and bake in a quick oven.—*Field and Fireside*, August 22, 1863

TO MAKE GOOD CHEESE CAKE. Take one quart of dry curd, mash it very fine and smooth. Take a quarter of a pound of butter, half a pint of cream—if you do not have cream, take milk—half a teaspoonful of salt, one nutmeg, six eggs, beat separately, and three-quarters of a pound of sugar. Mix well, if too thick, add milk; if too thin, one tablespoonful of corn starch. Bake in one crust. When made this way, they are a very desirable article.—*Southern Cultivator*, June 1861

PUFF PASTE. The art of making puff paste consists in keeping the dough firm and cool at the same time it is thoroughly kneaded. If it becomes at all warm and sticky, it will never be light. It should be skilfully handled, made in a cool place, and baked in a moderately quick oven.—*Farmer and Planter*, June 1861

THE CONFEDERATE HOUSEWIFE

CUSTARD PIES. Take five eggs, three cups of new milk, grated rinds and juice of three large lemons, five cups of sugar, and one tablespoonful of rice flour. Mix all well together, excepting the egg whites, which should be frisked until light and added last of all. Bake on rice crusts. This is enough for five pies.—*Farmer and Planter*, July 1861

TO MAKE PIE-MELON PIES. By Mrs. Dr. John Fisher, Columbia. Peel off the hard green rind, slice it, and remove the seed. Put it in a skillet, with just enough water to keep it from burning, with the grated peel of two lemons rubbed smoothly through a sieve or a colander. Sweeten and add the juice of the lemons. When about the consistency of apples for tarts, put it in a crust and bake it. When lemons cannot be obtained, citric acid may be used as a substitute.—*Farmer and Planter*, April 1861

SWEET POTATO PIE. Boil the potatoes very soft, then peel and mash them. To every quarter of a pound put one quart of milk, three tablespoonfuls of butter, and four beaten eggs, together with sugar and nutmeg to taste. It is improved with a glass of wine.—*Field and Fireside*, October 5, 1861

SWEET POTATO & VINEGAR PIE. Boil and slice five or six potatoes. Make a thin paste of wheat flour by mixing a tablespoonful with a little cold water first, then add boiling water. Sweeten and add vinegar to taste. Cover a soup plate with crust, putting in a layer of potato and several spoonfuls of sweetened paste alternately, then cover with an upper crust. A sauce of sweetened paste and vinegar, adding nutmeg, is usually served with the pie.—*Due-West Telescope*, September 20, 1861

CRACKER PIE. Eight crackers pounded fine, on which pour boiling water to soften. Add eight teaspoonfuls of vinegar, eight of sugar, and one of lemon. If too stiff, add water.—*Farmer and Planter*, August 1861

TOMATO PIE. The tomatoes are skinned and sliced, and after being mixed with sugar, are spiced and prepared in the same manner as other pies.

MOCK APPLE PIE. Over one and a half cups of bread crumbs, pour four cups of boiling water. Add one cup of sugar, one grated nutmeg, small pieces of butter, and an egg well beaten. Bake with two crusts. This is an excellent substitute when apples are scarce.

PUMPKIN PIE. Halve the pumpkin, take out the seeds, wash it clean, and cut it into small pieces. These are to be stewed gently until soft, then drained, and strained through a sieve. To one quart of the pulp, add three pints of cream or milk, six beaten eggs, together with sugar, mace, nutmeg, and ginger to taste. When the ingredients are well mixed, pour them upon pie plates having a bottom crust and bake forty minutes in a hot oven.—*Field and Fireside*, January 31, 1863

Family Dinners, May 1862

Here in Columbia the family dinners are the specialty. You call or they pick you up and drive home with you— "Oh, stay to dinner." And you stay gladly. They send for your husband. And he comes willingly. Then comes apparently a perfect dinner. You do not see how it could be improved. And they have not had time to alter things or add—because of the additional guests. They have every thing of the best. Silver, glass, china— table linen—damask—&c. &c. And then the planters live 'within themselves' as they call it— From the plantations come Mutton, Beef, poultry, cream, butter, eggs—fruits and vegetables. It is easy to live here—with a cook who has been sent to the best eating house in Charleston to trained— Old Mr. Chestnut's Romeo was apprenticed at Jones in town. I do not know where Mrs. Prestons got his degree, but he deserves a medal.

—Mary Boykin Chesnut Diary

CREAM CUSTARD. Mix a pint of cream with one of milk. Add five beaten eggs, a tablespoonful of flour, three of sugar, and nutmeg to taste. Mix and bake in cups or pie plates in a quick oven.—*Field and Fireside*, June 27, 1863

A PLAIN CUSTARD. Boil a pint of new milk, keeping a little back to mix with a tablespoonful of flour. Thicken the milk with the flour, let it cool a little, then add one egg well beaten. Sweeten to taste. Set on [the] fire again and stir until the egg turns, but do not let it boil. A little lemon or almond may be added.—*Field and Fireside*, January 10, 1863

RECIPE FOR MOLASSES CUSTARD. Beat all together, one cup of syrup or molasses, one cup of brown sugar, four eggs, and one tablespoon of butter. As soon as the custard is removed from the oven, moisten a little sugar with water and spread evenly over the top of the custard. Bake it in one crust. Try it, and you will be very apt to try it again, whenever molasses gets down to a reasonable price.—*Southern Recorder*, November 25, 1862

APPLE CUSTARD. To make the cheapest and best everyday farmer's apple custard, take sweet apples that will cook. Pare, cut, and stew them. When well done, stir till the pieces are broken. When cool, thin with milk to a proper consistency and bake with one crust like a pumpkin pie. Eggs may be prepared and added with the milk, if handy, though it will do without. No sweetening is necessary. It may be seasoned with any kind of spice to suit the taste, the less the better.—*Field and Fireside,* June 6, 1863

CODDLED APPLES. Take fall apples, wash, and put half a peck in a preserving kettle. Add half a cup of water sweetened with a large cup of sugar and half a cup of molasses. Cover and boil gently until tender.—*Field and Fireside,* June 13, 1863

JUMBLES. Three pounds of flour, two of sugar, one of butter, eight eggs, and a little caraway seed. Add a little milk, if the eggs are not sufficient, and bake.—*Field and Fireside,* March 21, 1863

A DELICATE DESSERT. Lay half a dozen crackers in a tureen. Cover with boiling water. In a few minutes they will be swollen to three or four times their original size. Grate loaf sugar and a little nutmeg over them. Dip on enough sweet cream to make a nice sauce, and you will have a delicious and simple dessert that will rest lightly upon the stomach—and it is easily prepared. Leave out the cream and it is a valuable recipe for sick room cookery.—*Field and Fireside,* February 21, 1863

RICE FLOUR BLANC MANGE. Boil one quart of milk, season it to your taste with sugar and rose water. Take four tablespoonfuls of rice flour, mix very smooth with cold water, and add this to the milk while it is boiling, stirring it well. Let all boil together about fifteen minutes, stirring occasionally, then pour into moulds and put it by to cool. This is a very favorite article for invalids.—*Clarke's Confederate Household Almanac,* 1863

CALVES' FEET BLANC MANGE. Boil four feet in five quarts of water, without any salt. When the liquor is reduced to one quart, strain and mix with one quart of milk. Add several sticks of cinnamon or vanilla beans. Boil ten minutes and sweeten to taste with white sugar. Strain it and fill your moulds.—*Field and Fireside,* May 16, 1863

DOUGHNUTS. To one pound of flour, put one quarter of a pound of butter, one quarter of a pound of sugar, and two spoonfuls of yeast. Mix all together in warm milk or water to a thickness of bread. Let rise and make into what form you please. Boil your lard and put them in.—*Field and Fireside,* February 14, 1863

TAPIOCA JELLY. Take a quarter of a pound of tapioca and wet it thoroughly in a pint of water. Then add a glass of wine, with sugar to taste. — *McLeod Journal*

Candles, Soaps, Cleaning & Dyeing

TALLOW CANDLES. Boil twenty pounds of tallow and two pounds of wax together in a very weak lye for about six hours. Turn out in a tub of cold water and let remain as a hard cake. Dissolve two pounds of alum in a bucket of water, put in the tallow, and again boil six hours. Then mould and use. The candles are firm and white.—*Field and Fireside,* December 14, 1861

WICKS FOR CANDLES. Prepare your wicks about half the usual size, wet with spirits of turpentine, put them in the sun to dry, and then mould or dip your candles. Candles thus made last longer and give a much clearer light. In fact, they are nearly or quite equal to sperm in clearness of light.—*Edgefield Advertiser,* November 6, 1861

TO REMOVE CANDLE GREASE FROM WINDOW GLASS. If all those who are thus troubled will wash the windows in a little turpentine, they will find the difficulty speedily removed.—*Farmer and Planter,* June 1861

TO WHITEN TALLOW. Melt the tallow and add a little alum and saltpetre, or a little nitric or sulphuric acid.—*Edgefield Advertiser,* March 22, 1862

CANDLES. Candles are the *vocative wanting* in the present declension of home comforts. But we do very well without them, so long as the postmaster can get a little piece from time to time to see how to open the mails. We have plenty of lightwood chunks—we split them into sticks of convenient size—we throw one on the fire after another—we have light enough to talk by until eight o'clock—we go to bed at a wise hour—and we get up early, prepared to use our daylight to good purpose. What's the use of grumbling about candles? They are no more essential than coffee or sugar. The absence of them may, in fact, be considered positively beneficial in some respects. The girls can't ruin their eyes and health now, reading novels until eleven o'clock P.M.—the older ladies can't sit sacrificing themselves at needle-work half the night—the parson can't get up such grand specimens of heavy prose. "Give us but light" is our cry—but let it be the glorious light of God's blessed sunshine, and this rightly used.—*Southern Cultivator,* July–August 1862

CANDLES FOR WAR TIMES, MADE WITH ROSIN. A model economical candle, sixty yards long, for use of soldiers in camp, which will burn six hours each night for six months, and all that light at a cost of a few cents, is

THE CONFEDERATE HOUSEWIFE

made as follows: Take one pound of beeswax and three-fourths of a pound of rosin. Melt them together, then take about four threads of slack-twisted cotton for a wick, and draw it about three times through the melted wax and rosin, and wind it in a ball. Pull the end up, and you have a good candle.—Porcher, *Resources, 500*

LARD CANDLES. To every eight pounds of lard, add one ounce of nitric acid in this manner. Having carefully weighed your lard, place it over a slow fire, or at least merely melt it. Then add the acid, mould the same as tallow, and you have a clear, beautiful candle. In order to make them resemble bona-fide tallow candles, you have only to add a small portion of pure beeswax.—*Field and Fireside*, October 4, 1862

MYRTLE WAX CANDLES. Boil berries of the myrtle, skim the wax from the pot, and treat as common wax or tallow in making candles.—*Charleston Daily Courier*, January 14, 1863

TO MAKE A GOOD LIGHT. Take a cup of grease of any kind (lard or tallow) and into it put a sycamore ball, saturate in the same, and then light it—you have a light superior to candles. One ball will last three or four nights. The expense will be about three cents a night, till usual bed time—not more, even at the present prices of tallow.—*Field and Fireside*, June 27, 1863

TO MAKE TALLOW CANDLES HARD. Take the leaf of the prickly pear, say four or five, cut up, and boil with one pound of tallow, and your candles will surprise you with their hardness.

TO MAKE MUTTON SUET CANDLES. Throw quick lime into melted mutton suet. The lime will fall to the bottom and carry along with it all the dirt of the suet, so as to leave it as pure and as fine as wax itself. Now, if to one part of the suet you mix three of real wax, you will have a very fine, and to appearance, a real wax candle, at least the mixture could never be discovered, not even in the moulding way of ornaments.—*Clarke's Confederate Household Almanac*, 1863

TO MAKE FAMILY SOAP. Take six pounds of bar soap, one quarter of a pound of sal soda, three teaspoonfuls of spirits of turpentine, one and one-half teaspoonfuls of camphor, and two teaspoonfuls of salt. Cut the soap up fine, boil the water, and all the ingredients. Boil thirty minutes. Take off and pour into shallow vessels to cool and harden. Or, take five pounds of bar soap, four pounds of sal soda, two ounces of borax, and one ounce of hartshorn. Dissolve in twenty-two quarts of soft water and boil fifteen to twenty minutes.

TO MAKE JELLY SOAP. After pouring out of the vessel the above, pour in water to wash off the sides and bottom and boil twenty minutes. Then pour off to cool, and you have elegant jelly soap for washing clothes, etc.

TO MAKE SOFT SOAP. Take ten pounds of potash well pulverized, fifteen pounds of grease, and three buckets of boiling water. Mix and stir potash and water together until dissolved. Then add the grease, stirring well. Put all in a barrel, and every morning add two buckets of cold water, stirring it well each time, until the barrel is nearly full or mixed to the consistency of soft soap.—*Edgefield Advertiser*, November 6, 1861

CORN SHUCK SOAP. Take one gallon of strong lye. Add half a pound of shucks cut up fine. Let the shucks boil in the lye until they are reduced to shreds. Then fish the shreds out and put in a half a pound of crackling grease, or six ounces of lard. Boil until sufficiently thick to make a good soap.—*Field and Fireside*, March 6, 1862

SOAP WITHOUT GREASE. To four gallons of strong lye, add ten pounds of distilled rosin or eight pounds of fine gum, not distilled and free

77

from trash is better. Boil steadily until there is no rosin to be seen. If the quantity of lye is not sufficient, add more and continue to add until the rosin is out, and boil until it makes a brown jelly soap. I have used this soap for a year, and it is equal to the best soap made with grease.—*McLeod Journal*

COTTON SEED SOAP. Put cotton seed into a large and strong iron pot, in small quantities at a time, mash them well with a wooden pestle, and then pour in a certain quantity of common lye and boil thoroughly. Strain in an ordinary sieve, and proceed in the usual way of drying and cutting into cakes. The oil is thus yielded and saponified.—Porcher, *Resources*, 97

A SIMPLE METHOD OF MAKING SOAP. To thirty-two gallons of ley, of strength just sufficient to bear an egg, add sixteen pounds of clean, melted grease, which, by being placed in the hot sun, and occasionally stirred, will, in a few days, produce a soap of the first quality. Use hard soap to wash clothes and soft to wash floors.—*Confederate States Almanac,* 1865

HOME MADE SOAP AND STARCH. A lady sends us the following simple and useful recipe for making soap and starch: Put up the bones of everything for a fortnight, and then boil them in strong lye, skimming as long as the grease rises. The next day boil the grease with strong lye until it becomes soap. Put some lime in the lye barrel, and it makes much better soap. All of my starch is soft hominy or gruel strained. If you have not come to it yet, try it. How much this war will teach us.—*Charleston Mercury,* May 6, 1862

HOME-MADE STARCH. In the present state of the corn, as good starch can be made of it as any housewife needs. Grate it from the ear, mix the pulp thoroughly with cold water, and strain it through a sieve. Let the liquor settle and, pouring off the water, which will be discolored, the starch will be found at the bottom of the vessel in a rather soft cake. Pour on more water, stir it up, and repeat the process. At each repetition, the cake will be found firmer. And when the water comes off clear and the starch is free from a pink or yellow tinge on the top, the process is complete, except for drying. I never knew but one miscarriage, and that was in warm weather, when the water was not cold enough, or was allowed to stand too long, and the mass fermented. A grater can be made from an old coffee pot or tin bucket, by punching it (outward) full of holes—a hammer and a nail will answer the purpose—and tacking it to a piece of board.—*Field and Fireside,* February 7, 1863

STARCH POLISH. Take one ounce of spermaceti and one ounce of white wax. Melt and run it into a thin cake on a plate. A piece the size of a quarter, added to a quart of prepared starch, gives a beautiful lustre to the clothes and prevents the iron from sticking.—*Field and Fireside,* February 14, 1863

STARCH. In making starch from wheat, the grain is steeped in cold water until it becomes soft and yields a milky juice by pressure. It is then put into sacks of linen and pressed in a vat filled with cold water, as long as any milky juice exudes. After standing some time, the fluid gradually becomes clear, and a white powder, which is starch, remains at the bottom.—*Confederate States Almanac, 1864*

SUBSTITUTE FOR GUM ARABIC. Gum Arabic is used in some cases to increase the strength and brilliancy of starch. For fine clothes, the gum which exudes from plum, peach, or cherry trees, when transparent, answers the purpose well. For making and sealing envelopes, the gum from the common red cherry tree is a good substitute for Gum Arabic.—*Charleston Mercury,* January 17, 1863

ECONOMY IN LINEN WASHING. A small quantity of clay pipe dissolved in water employed for washing gives the dirtiest linens the appearance of having been bleached and cleans them thoroughly with about one-half of the labor and a saving of fully one-fourth of the soap.—*Field and Fireside,* February 21, 1863

WASHING FLANNELS. Make hot suds—with good soft soap. Put in the flannels and let them lie a few minutes, then wash thoroughly with the hands. Have ready some boiling water, dissolve a little blueing, or indigo, and pour on it sufficient of the hot water to improve the goods. Put them in and let them remain until cool enough to wring. Dry in the air and iron when slightly damp. Iron on the right side.—*Spartanburg Express,* February 19, 1862

FRUIT STAINS IN LINEN. To remove them, rub the part on each side with yellow soap, then tie up a piece of pearlash in the cloth and soak well in hot water or boil. Afterwards expose the stained part to the sun and air until removed.—*Field and Fireside,* February 7, 1863

TO REMOVE GRASS STAINS FROM WOOLEN CLOTHES. Place a rag of several thicknesses under the stained spot. Saturate another rag with ether and rub the spot until the stain disappears.—*Field and Fireside,* June 6, 1863

TO CLEAN SILK. Pare and slice thin three washed Irish potatoes. Pour on them a half a pint of boiling water and let it stand till it is cold. Strain the water and add an equal quantity of alcohol. Sponge the silk on the right side and, when half done, iron it on the wrong side. The lightest color silk may be cleaned and brightened by this process, also cloth velvet and crape.—*McLeod Journal*

TO CLEAN GOLD LACE. Gold lace is easily cleaned and restored to its original brightness by rubbing it with a soft brush dipped in roche alum burnt, sifted to a very fine powder.

TO CLEAN GLOVES WITHOUT WETTING THEM. Lay the gloves upon a clean board, make a mixture of dried fulling earth and powdered alum, and pass them over on each side with a common stiff brush. Sweep it

THE CONFEDERATE HOUSEWIFE

off. Sprinkle with dry bran and whiting and dust well. This, if they be not exceedingly greasy, will render them quite clean. If they are still soiled, take out the grease with toasted bread crumbs and powder of burnt bone. Then pass them over with a woolen cloth dipped in fulling earth or alum powder. In this manner, they can be cleaned without wetting, which frequently shrinks and spoils them.—*Field and Fireside,* January 10, 1863

INK STAINS ON MAHOGANY. Put a few drops of spirits of nitre in a teaspoonful of water, touch the spot with a feather dipped in the mixture, and on the ink disappearing, rub it over immediately with a rag wetted in cold water, or there will be a white mark which will not be easily effaced.—*Southern Confederacy,* March 12, 1861

TO TAKE INK OUT OF LINEN. Take a piece of tallow, melt it, and dip the spotted part of the linen into the tallow. The linen may be washed, and the spot will disappear, the linen remaining uninjured.—*Field and Fireside,* January 2, 1864

TO TAKE STAINS OUT OF SILVER. Steep the silver in soap-lye for the space of four hours. Then cover with whiting, wet with vinegar, so that it may lie thick, and dry by a fire. After which, rub off the whiting and pass it over with dry bran, and the spots will not only disappear, but the silver will look exceedingly bright.—*Field and Fireside,* March 7, 1863

TO CLEAN MARBLE. Marble is best cleaned with a little soap and water to which some ox-gall may be added. Acids are to be avoided.—*Field and Fireside,* April 4, 1863

CLEANING KETTLES. A bit of pearlash as large as a walnut, dissolved in hot water, will remove grease from iron cooking vessels and also take out the taste left by onions or other highly flavored foods.—*Field and Fireside,* April 11, 1863

TO CLEAN A BRASS KETTLE. Use salt and vinegar, before cooking in it.—*Confederate States Almanac,* 1864

SCOURING KNIVES. A small, clean potato, with the end cut off, is a very convenient medium of applying brick dust to knives, keeping it at about the right moisture while the juice of the potato assists in removing stains from the surface. We get a better polish by this method than by any other we have tried, and with less labor.—*Field and Fireside,* January 31, 1863

TO PRESERVE POLISHED STEEL. Grind an ounce of native plumbago (such as is used in making lead pencils) very fine in a gill of spirits of turpentine. Add an ounce of beeswax and apply a gentle heat till the wax is melted. Then stir until the mixture is nearly cold and apply to the steel with a brush. When the spirits have evaporated, rub the work hard with a piece of glove leather and wipe off nearly all of the wax so that the metal may retain

JOHN HAMMOND MOORE

its brightness. This process may be applied to iron or steel in machinery, or other work, and will be found to answer a much better purpose than oil, as it is less liable to collect dust from the atmosphere and is, in general, more durable.—*Field and Fireside*, July 11, 1863

COPPERAS AS A DISINFECTING AGENT. A couple of pounds dissolved in ten pounds of water and poured in offensive place.—*McLeod Journal*

SUBSTITUTE FOR COPPERAS. We have received from good authority, says the *Macon Journal and Messenger*, the following recipe: Half pint vinegar, half pint syrup of molasses, three gallons of water. Put in an iron pot with nails or other rusty iron and let stand twenty days. It is no use buying copperas or dyeing at one dollar per pound while this will answer every purpose.—*Field and Fireside*, April 23, 1864

CHEAP, BUT GOOD BLACKING. A friend has suggested to us a receipt for making blacking, which he says can be recommended both on account of its cheapness and its quality. To a teacup of molasses stir in lampblack until it is black. Then add the white of an egg, well beaten, and to this add a pint of vinegar or whiskey, and put in a bottle for use. Shake it before using. This experiment is at least worth a trial, as the price of ordinary blacking has so rapidly advanced since the blockade. A neatly polished boot is as much an ornament to the person of any man or woman, as much indeed, as a clean shirt bosom or collar.—*Carolina Spartan*, May 1, 1862

BLACKING FROM CHINA BERRIES. The *Columbus Sun* recommends its readers to preserve the following recipe: If you want good blacking, take a half bushel of China berries, and having them well picked from the stems, put into a kettle, and add three gallons of water; boil down to one gallon, then strain the liquor, through a sieve, from the seeds and skins, and add as much pine wood soot (the richer the better) as will make a good black, and it is ready for use. A pint of good or a quart of weak vinegar (or stale beer), first mixed with the soot, will make it better, and if you add the whole of one egg to a half gallon of the liquor it will best and equal any Yankee blacking. This blacking costs little besides trouble; and we have seen boots cleaned with it inferior to none in gloss, and it will not soil a white handkerchief. Let stand several days before you bottle it.—*Southern Confederacy*, May 16, 1863

BLACK WAX. Dissolve wax—either yellow or white—and stir in soot until it is very black. Let it cool, and you have an article that will be quite useful while black thread is so scarce.—*Field and Fireside*, February 21, 1863

RECIPE FOR DYEING SLATE COLORS. Boil equal parts of the inside bark of sassafras and willow in a brass kettle. Strain the decoction from the bark and add to the fluid a small tablespoonful of copperas, the same of alum, or a small portion more of the latter. Have the wool well scoured and

81

taken out of the clean soap suds. Wring it dry and put it into the dye—let it boil a short time, raising it out to get air frequently. Dry it and then wash it in suds until quite cleansed from the smell of dye. It is a permanent color and it does not take a great quantity of the bark named. A black jack bark will also dye a good slate color, prepared in the same way, but it is not so permanent a color.

RECIPE FOR DYEING SKY BLUE. Take any old green ribbon or silk and boil it in a brass kettle until the color is extracted. Add to the water a little alum—wash the yarn or silk in clean suds. Put it in the dye, boil a few minutes, and dry it. It may be washed in cold water before it is dried.

TO DYE YELLOW. Take broom straw, cut up in short pieces, about four or five inches long, boil in clear water in a brass kettle. Add alum until it curdles, then drain it and let it settle. The stalks should be taken out before the alum is put in, and it should settle after straining before the articles are put in. This dyes silk or wool, and cotton also, but not so clear a yellow.

TO DYE BROWN. The sassafras prepared as the slate above, add only the copperas, will dye a beautiful brown. This is for wool, but may dye cotton. Anything that will color wool will also color silk, but not always cotton. It is

---

In Sherman's Wake

November 16, 1864 — As I could not obtain in Covington what I went for in the way of dye stuffs, etc., I concluded this morning, in accordance with Mrs. Ward's wish, to go to the Circle [Social Circle]. We took Old Dutch and had a pleasant ride as it was a delightful day, but how dreary looks the town! Where formerly all was bustle and business, now naked chimneys and bare walls, for the depot and surroundings were all burned by last summer's raiders. Engaged to sell some bacon and potatoes. Obtained my dye stuffs. Paid seven dollars . . . a pound for coffee, six dollars an ounce for indigo, twenty dollars for a quire of paper, five dollars for ten cents' worth of flax thread, six dollars for pins, and forty dollars for a bunch of factory thread.

—Burge, *Wartime Journal*, 15–16

not much trouble to try it.—*Edgefield Advertiser*, July 30, 1862

CONFEDERATE DYE. To make a beautiful blue, take elderberries, mash them, and press out the juice. To two gallons of juice add about one ounce of copperas and two ounces of alum. Dip the thread in this thoroughly, air, and the dye is set.—*Clarke's Confederate Household Almanac*, 1863

TO DYE CRIMSON. To two gallons of the juice of pokeberries, when they are quite ripe, add half a gallon of strong cider vinegar, to dye one pound of wool, which must be first washed very clean with hard soap. The wool, when wrung dry, is to be put into the vinegar and pokeberry juice, and simmered in a copper kettle for one hour. Then take it out, let it drip a while, and spread it in the sun. The vessel must be free of grease of any kind.—*Confederate States Almanac*, 1864

THE CONFEDERATE HOUSEWIFE

Additional Advice
for Mistress & Servant

ABOUT THE HOME. If your flat-irons are rough, rub them with fine salt. If you are buying a carpet for durability, choose small figures. A hot shovel held over varnished furniture will take out white spots. A small piece of glue dissolved in skim milk and water will restore old crape. Ribbons should be washed in cold suds and not rinsed. Scotch snuff put into holes where crickets come out will destroy them.—*Farmer and Planter*, August 1861

HOUSEHOLD MEASURES. As all families are not provided with scales or weights, here are those for ingredients in general use by every housewife:

Weights and Measures
Wheat flour, 1 pound = 1 quart.
Indian meal, 1 pound, 2 ounces = 1 quart.
Butter, when soft, 1 pound, 1 ounce = 1 quart.
Loaf sugar, broken, 1 pound = 1 quart.
White sugar, powdered, 1 pound, 1 ounce = 1 quart.
Best brown sugar, 1 pound, 2 ounces = 1 quart.
Eggs, average size, 10 = 1 pound.

Liquid Measure
Sixteen tablespoonfuls = 1/2 pint.
Eight tablespoonfuls = 1 gill.
Four tablespoonfuls = 1/2 gill.
A common-sized tumbler holds 1/2 pint.
A common-sized wine glass holds 1/2 gill.
—*Edgefield Advertiser*, February 22, 1865

TO DRY HERBS. Gather them on a dry day, just before they begin to blossom. Brush off the dust, cut them in small branches, and dry them quickly in a moderate oven. Pick off the leaves when dry, pound and sift them, bottle immediately, and cork closely. They must be kept in a dry place.—*Edgefield Advertiser*, August 28, 1861

KITCHEN ODORS. A skilled housekeeper says that the unpleasant odor arising from boiling ham, cabbage, &c., is completely corrected by throw-

JOHN HAMMOND MOORE

ing whole red peppers into the pot—at the same time the flavor of the food is improved. It is said that pieces of charcoal will produce the same effect. —*Field and Fireside,* April 4, 1863

ECONOMICAL USE OF NUTMEG. If a person begins to grate a nutmeg at the stalk end, it will prove hollow throughout; whereas the same nutmeg, grated at the other end, would have proved sound and solid to the last. This circumstance may thus be accounted for: The centre of a nutmeg consists of a number of fibres issuing from the stalk and its continuation through the centre of the fruit, the other ends of which fibres, though closely surrounded and pressed by the fruit, do not adhere to it. When the stalk is grated away, those fibres, having lost their hold, gradually drop out in succession, and the hollow continues throughout the whole nut. By beginning at the contrary end, the fibres above mentioned are grated off at their core end, with the surrounding fruit, and do not drop out and cause a hole.—*Field and Fireside,* March 21, 1863

SAVE THE ROSE LEAVES. Rose leaves are extensively used in the manufacture of blue pills, and are in great demand for preparing this valuable medicine. The gardens of city and country now abound in roses, and we are sure that the ladies will see that the leaves are made to subserve this purpose of utility. Surgeon J. J. Chisholm, of the Medical Purveying Department, in Columbia, S.C., invokes the aid of ladies in collecting a supply, and we trust our lady readers everywhere will heartily respond to the call.—*Southern Watchman,* June 17, 1863

SUBSTITUTE FOR SODA. To the ashes of corn cobs add a little boiling water. After allowing it to stand for a few minutes, pour off the lye, which can be used at once with an acid, such as milk or vinegar. It makes the bread as light almost as soda.—*Clarke's Confederate Household Almanac,* 1863

TO PURIFY SORGHUM FOR TABLE USE. Pour a gallon and a half of syrup into preserving kettles, add the beaten whites of two eggs (half a pint or little over of sweet milk may be substituted for the eggs), a small teaspoonful of cooking soda, and two quarts of water. Stir well together and bring them to the boiling point. Remove all the scum as it rises. When it boils, strain it, and boil it down again to a thick syrup. If all the acidity is not removed, add more soda. A fine clear article is thus produced, much richer in sweetness than ordinary syrup. Old West Indian and New Orleans syrup are vastly improved by the same process. Prepare it from time to time and use it while fresh. Try it.—*Edgefield Advertiser,* February 22, 1865

CARE OF OIL CLOTH. When an oil cloth begins to lose its brightness of coloring, we have found a coat of varnish the best thing for the process of restoration. Cleanse by washing the surface. We have never heard of any application of oil.—*Field and Fireside,* June 6, 1863

THE CONFEDERATE HOUSEWIFE

TO MAKE CANVAS. Take thick, smooth, strong cotton or linen cloth. Wet and stretch and tack on a frame. When dry, apply white lead mixed with linseed oil to the consistency of dough. Spread this mixture on the stretched cloth and smooth with a palette knife. Put it by to dry and in a week it will be ready for use. Allow me to add that if an interesting picture be painted on the cloth it will form a cheap and elegant screen for the fireplace.—*Field and Fireside,* March 7, 1863

TO MAKE CLOTH WATER-PROOF WITH TURPENTINE. In making cloth water-proof for negroes in picking cotton when the weed is wet from rain or dews, and also for tents, the following method is adopted: To every gallon of spirits of turpentine put two and a half pounds of beeswax, boil well in a pot, remove from the fire, and while it is hot put on the goods. Move it about until it is well saturated, then hang it up to dry. It will require one gallon of turpentine to every eight yards of goods. It is more pliant than India-rubber.—Porcher, *Resources,* 500

CLOTHING FOR SOLDIERS. All who can do should, at the earliest possible day, make up something like the following for their friends and relatives, omitting such, of course, as have heretofore been furnished: Two pair of pants of heavy brown or grey mixed jeans, lined, if thought advisable, with domestic. One roundabout, or army jacket, of the same material, lined throughout, with side and vest pockets. It should be long enough to cover some four inches below the waistband of the pants and large enough to be worn over the vest or outside shirt. One heavy vest of jeans, linsey, or kersey. One overshirt, of some woolen or mixed. One or two pair of drawers, as they may require. Two pair of heavy woolen socks. One good blanket—lined is advisable. An overcoat or hunting shirt with a belt.—*Southern Watchman,* August 28, 1861

THE COMFORT CLOAK—A SUBSTITUTE FOR OVERCOATS AND BLANKETS FOR OUR ARMY. Take a sufficient quantity of common shirting, dye it brown with the black walnut, cut it, and make it in the form of a large, loose cloak, *without sleeves,* leaving slits for the arms. Wad it with cotton batting, in thin layers like a quilt, fix an oil cape on it, reaching down to the waist, the throat and breast part to be fastened with strings—and you have the most complete cloak and blanket ever slept in, and much lighter than a woolen coat. The object of the oil cloth cape is to protect the garment as well as the arms from the rain. The collar should be made wide so as to cover the ears and neck when raised.—*Yorkville Enquirer,* November 5, 1862

A VALUABLE SUGGESTION. If all of the ladies of the Southern States were to begin now and make the old negro women on the plantations knit coarse socks, a large supply might be ready, if we should have a winter campaign. On every plantation in the South, there is a large amount of labor which is of very little value, and by directing it into this channel, a want which will surely arise will be met.—*Southern Cultivator*, July 1861

Hard Times in Atlanta

June 22, 1863 — Have done nothing but mend to-day. The hard times give me plenty of that kind of amusement. Shirting is three dollars a yard, but S[ylvanus] will soon have to buy some for shirts. Patching and darning will not avail much longer to keep a shirt on his back. I am knitting me a pair of confederate hose. I never wore coarse unbleached stockings before but am thankful to get them now. The cotton to knit with was a present from Sister when I was in Columbus. She is always giving me something useful. Ladies' white cotton hose are only $3 a pair; just such ones as I have bought at the North for 15 c{e}nts.

—Jennie Akehurst Diary

TO KNIT HEELS. To knit the heels of socks double, so that they may last twice as long as otherwise, skip every alternate stitch on the wrong side and knit all on the right. This will make it double, like that of a double-ply, ingrain carpet.—*Edgefield Advertiser*, November 5, 1862

CONFEDERATE MATCHES. Take strips of wood and dip them into melted sulphur, and let them dry, which will be done in a minute after dipping them. Then the points of these sulphured matches must be dipped in a composition made in the following manner, viz: Dissolve in hot water, gum arabic, four parts, chlorate of potassa, one part, and phosphorus, one part. These are to be added to the hot water separately, and in the order herein prescribed. As soon as the first ingredient is dissolved, then add the second, &c., until all is dissolved. This must be done in a warm bath (like glue is prepared), and the mixture must be kept in the water bath while the process of dipping is going on. The matches are to be thoroughly dried before they are used. Dry in the shade for twenty-four hours. Cover the mixture closely.—*Southern Cultivator*, September–October 1862

CONFEDERATE PINS. A few evenings since, a gentleman laughingly remarked that he had seen a lady using what she called Confederate pins. These consisted of thorns of the large cactus or prickly pear, which is furnished by nature with both head and point. It is well known that during the Revolutionary War of our fathers, the thorns of the plum tree were used for the same purposes. Buttons of almost any size may be extemporized from the hard shell of the gourd, cut and covered with cloth. If anything harder or more durable is required, it can be made of horn, boiled until it is soft, and then trimmed with a knife to the proper size, and bored.—*Southern Cultivator*, March–April 1863

HOW TO MAKE A COAL FIRE. If everybody knew how to make a good coal fire, there would be more comfort inside and less smoke outside the houses in cold weather. Before you throw on the coals, pull all the fire to the front of the grate toward the bars, fill up the cavity at the back with cinders and ashes, which will be found under the grate, then throw on the coals. The gas evolved in the process of roasting the coal will be absorbed by the cinders and render them in an increasing degree combustible. The smoke will thus be burnt, and a fine, glowing, smokeless fire will be the result.—*Southern Confederacy*, March 18, 1861

SOOT IN CHIMNEYS. By taking fire and dropping cinders on dry shingle roofs, soot causes many conflagrations. Most fires in the country originate in this way. Be particular to clean or burn out soot at least once a year, when the roof is wet.—*Edgefield Advertiser*, November 5, 1862

FIRES. Housekeepers cannot be too constant and vigilant in impressing on all servants the importance of attention to fire and fireplaces. From the increased use of wood instead of coal, the dangers of accidental fires from ashes, or flues or chimneys, have been increased and should be accordingly watched.—*Charleston Daily Courier*, December 20, 1862

TO REMOVE CLINKERS FROM STOVES. Put a few oyster shells into the grate while the fire is ignited. The clinkers will become loosened so as to be readily removed without the danger of breaking the lining. We have tried this remedy; and, while the chemical action is involved in mystery, it accomplished the result to our satisfaction.—*Field and Fireside*, April 4, 1863

TO MEND CRACKS IN STOVES. Take equal parts of wood ashes and common salt, and mix them to a proper consistence with water; with this fill the cracks.—*Edgefield Advertiser*, April 17, 1861

HOW TO MAKE CHIMNEYS FOR KEROSENE OR PALMETTO OIL LAMPS. Take a common sweet-oil bottle, cut off the bottom by burning a string wet with turpentine around the bottle. Then make a bottom of tin to fit the lamp, fasten it to the bottle with plaster of Paris, and you have as good a chimney as you can buy. This is something worth knowing at the present time. When one chimney breaks, the same tin bottom will do for another.—*Field and Fireside*, November 8, 1862

TO PREVENT SMOKE FROM A LAMP. Soak the wick in strong vinegar and dry well before use. It will burn sweet and pleasant and give much satisfaction for the trifling trouble of preparing it.—*Field and Fireside*, April 11, 1863

TO MAKE ECONOMICAL WICKS FOR LAMPS. When using a lamp with a flat wick, if you take a piece of clean cotton stocking it will answer the purpose as well as the cotton wicks that are sold in the shops.—*Edgefield Advertiser*, November 5, 1862

TUMBLERS CHEAP. Take a claret bottle, or any kind of glass bottle—bottles of thin white glass with flat bottoms are the best. Hold the bottle firmly by both ends. Let another person, having a cup of water ready, pass a stout cotton cord twice around the bottle and create a friction by pulling the ends of the cord to and fro for a minute or so. Then let him jerk the cord off, dash the water on quickly, and presto! you hold in one hand as serviceable a tumbler or goblet as you need wish, and in the other a neat but not gaudy glass candlestick! The bottle should be held with a strap, piece of leather, or some substance with a hard, straight edge, firmly around it at the intended point of severance, in order to keep the cord in place during the friction and secure straight and smooth edges in the glassware. Old bottles can be put to good use in this way.—*Edgefield Advertiser*, November 23, 1864

TO EXTRACT A GLASS STOPPER. Take a large strip of wool, pass it around the neck of the bottle, and attach one end of this to a board or some fixed object. Hold the other, and see-saw the bottle along it. The friction will soon heat the neck of the bottle, and by the heat, the neck will expand sufficiently to allow of the stopper being extracted.

TO TOUGHEN EARTHENWARE. It is a good plan to put new earthenware into cold water, and let it heat gradually until it boils, and then cools again. Brown earthenware, in particular, may be toughened in this way. A handful of rye, or wheat bran, thrown in while it is boiling, will prevent acid or salt from destroying the glazing.

CHINESE METHOD OF MENDING CHINA. Take a piece of flint glass, beat it to a fine powder, and grind it with the white of an egg. This mixture joins china without riveting, so that no act can break it in the same place. This composition is to be ground finely on a painter's stone. This simple method is recommended to all who have broken china, now that it is impossible to replace it.

TO MEND BROKEN CHINA OR GLASSWARE. Pound burned oyster shells, sift the powder through a very fine sieve, and grind it on a painter's stone till it becomes very fine. Then take the whites of several eggs, according to the quantity of the powder, beat them well, and having mixed them with it, form the whole into a kind of paste. Join the pieces of china or glass with a bit of paste, press them together for seven or eight minutes, and the united pieces will stand heat and water, and will not come apart if they should fall to the ground.—*Confederate States Almanac,* 1865

JOINING GLASS. Melt a little isinglass in spirits of wine and add a small quantity of water. Warm the mixture gently over a moderate fire. When mixed thoroughly by melting, it will form a glue perfectly transparent and reunite broken glass so nicely and firmly that the joining will scarcely be perceptible to the most critical eye. Lime mixed with the white of an egg also forms a very strong cement for glass, porcelain, &c., but it must be neatly done; and, when hard, the superfluous part cannot readily be smoothed down or taken off.—*Field and Fireside,* March 28, 1863

TO MEND IRON POTS. Mix finely silted lime with some white of an egg till a thick kind of paste is formed. Add some iron filings, apply to the fracture, and the vessel will be found to be nearly as sound as ever.—*Field and Fireside,* March 7, 1863

TO POLISH MAHOGANY TABLES. Grate very fine a quarter of an ounce of white soap and put it into a glazed earthen vessel with a pint of water. Hold it over a fire till the soap is dissolved. Then add the same quantity of white wax cut up into small pieces and three ounces of common wax. As soon as the whole is incorporated, it is fit for use. When used, clean the table well, dip a bit of flannel in the varnish when warm, and rub it on the table; let stand a quarter of an hour and then apply a hard brush in all directions. Finish with a bit of clean flannel. This will produce a gloss like a mirror and, to those who dislike the smell of turpentine or oil, will be found most valuable.—*Field and Fireside,* February 21, 1863

TO PREVENT MOULD IN BOOKS. A few drops of oil of lavender will save a library from mould.—*Field and Fireside,* March 7, 1863

CHEAP INK. We write this paragraph, says the *Wilmington (N.C.) Journal,* with a very black, free flowing ink, made by boiling in water the bark of the bay or dwarf magnolia, cut into small pieces. This ink appears to us to be equal in every respect to any other we have seen, and is easily made from a material obtainable almost anywhere in the low country. It seems as though it would permanently retain color; at least, some writing done nearly a month ago looks blacker than it did at first.—*Southern Confederacy,* May 1, 1863

INDELIBLE INK. Green persimmons, say twelve of them, mash, and pour on water sufficient to cover them. Boil over a slow fire, but do not boil too much. Then add a small piece of copperas. This ink cannot be rubbed out and will not change color.—*Yorkville Enquirer,* October 7, 1863

FOR MAKING INK. Soft maple bark and willow bark, equal parts—a handful of each boiled in about four parts of water, reduced to one quart. Take out the bark and add a lump of copperas about the size of a man's thumb at the first joint. If on writing it, the ink appears very black, with a gloss on it, add a little water.—*Edgefield Advertiser,* July 30, 1863

TO FIND THE LENGTH OF ANY DAY IN THE YEAR. Simply multiply the time of the sun's setting by two.—*Miller's Planters' & Merchants' Almanac,* 1861

BEECH-TREE LEAVES. The leaves of the beech-tree, collected at autumn in dry weather, form an admirable article for filling beds for the poor. The smell is grateful and wholesome. They do not harbor vermin, are very elastic, and may be replenished annually without cost.—*Edgefield Advertiser,* November 5, 1862

RYE STRAW HATS. I saw an appeal in the *Charleston Courier* a short time ago to the ladies for some plan of manufacturing hats for summer wear, and as I have been quite successful in making pretty, light, and durable hats of "rye straw," which can be procured in all parts of the Confederacy, and made into hats by anyone, I send you the following directions for preparing it for use: Cut the rye when the grain is in "the milk," take off the tops, that is the grain, about a foot, then dip the rest in a large pot of boiling water, being careful that it all gets wet, spread thin in the hot sun, taking it in when it rains, as the texture of the straw is injured and causes it to mildew; leave it out night and day for eight or nine days, when it will be sufficiently white for use. You then cut it from joint to joint, removing the husk, then dip in water (warm or cold) to soften it (as you can do nothing with it in a dry state), split in half with a dull knife, or, better, the half of an old pair of scissors, and draw through a small machine made for the purpose by any machinist, and it is ready for plaiting.—A Lady of Camden, *Charleston Daily Courier,* June 9, 1864

USE OF RYE STRAW. In a recent issue of your paper, "A Lady of Camden" proposed a mode of making hats from rye straw—a specie of sombrero which I have seen, and to the usefullness of which, in sheltering the head from the heat of the sun, I can testify. There are many other good uses, however, to which rye straw may be applied besides making hats. Where the cereal grows plentifully the harness-maker finds no better material to stuff

THE CONFEDERATE HOUSEWIFE

his collars than with rye straw chopped up fine with a cutting-knife. The good housewife who puts down her own home-grown rag-carpet, finds nothing to put under it, to make it tread more softly, than good, clean, bright, slippery rye straw. Lastly, the straws of the rye cut just before it is fully ripened, may be made into most beautiful window curtains. I have seen curtains made of this material frequently, and I do not hesitate to pronounce them as ornamental as economical. The straw may be painted or dyed any color to suit the fancy, and a coat of varnish imparts to it a most brilliant appearance. They can be very easily made. Cut the straws of the same length, and loop them together, one by one, a few inches from each end and in the middle, until enough are fastened together for the purpose. At the places where the straws are sewn together pieces of gimp or ribbon should be tacked lengthwise, in order to conceal the threads. The edges and ends should be bound with any material to suit the taste, and ornamented with a fringe. The curtain is then attached to a roller, and sustained in the window. When the work is skillfully executed, these curtains made of homely rye straw do not lose much by comparison with Venetian blinds.—TRIPTOLOMUS, *Charleston Daily Courier*, June 18, 1864

WE HAVE MADE SEVEN OR EIGHT STRAW HATS

Yankees are as near here as they are to charleston so we are in as much danger in one place as another. We use wheat and rhy flour togather [sic] to make bread. We have made seven or eight straw hats [,] mother plaits them and alice and myself sew them [,] they pay us in vegetables, we got last night for one hat a bushel of corn meal.

**—S. Macdonald writing from Cherokee Ford
on the Broad River to Mrs. Mackenzie in Charleston,
September 18, 1864, Mackenzie Family Papers**

HOW TO MANUFACTURE SALT FOR HOME USE. Take a towel, or any piece of cloth—say, two yards long—sew the two ends together, hang it on a roller, and let one end revolve in a tub or basin of salt water; the sun and air will

JOHN HAMMOND MOORE

act on the cloth, and evaporate the water rapidly. It must be revolved several times throughout the day, so that the cloth is well saturated. When the solution is evaporated to near the bottom, dip from the concentrated brine, and pour it in a large flat dish or plate; let it remain in the sun until the salt is formed; taking it in every night, and placing a cover over it. This is accomplished by capillary attraction, and can be manufactured for $1 per sack, on a large scale. Each gallon of salt water will produce two and a half ounces of salt when evaporated. P. S. To make salt requires a little patience, as it is of slow formation. John Commins, Charleston Tannery.—*Charleston Mercury,* June 11, 1862

A WORD TO THE WISE. The *Tallahassee Sentinel* warns its readers of the folly of buying the dark and impure salt that is brought along the coast. It will not save meat but spoil it. We are informed that some of the salt-makers, who are making for market, make an inferior article, for which they charge six and eight dollars a bushel. It were better to give twelve dollars or more per bushel and get a good article, than to buy that which is comparatively worthless at half the price. If our people will refuse to buy the inferior article it will soon induce salt-makers to make a good salt. Pure salt is white, and that which is

---

My Salt Works Aren't Working

I am afraid my "salt works" are destined shortly to come to a close. I find the kettles are burning out. And indeed they are so small that it is impossible to make very pure salt with them. I have been going out constantly & directing operations; but I find it is not as white & dry as my neighbors, who have five or six large pans and kettles. These pans cost from <u>eight hundred</u> to <u>one thousand</u> dollars apiece. And I cannot afford to make any such investment now. They also employ from eight to ten hands, besides waggon & mules. I will try & send up some of the salt we have made this week for you to try.

—G. J. Kollock writing from Savannah to his wife in Clarkesville, Ga., February 16, 1863, in Kollock, ed., "Letters," September 1950, 252–53

---

best for saving meat is large-grained. A word to the wise is sufficient.—*Southern Confederacy*, August 28, 1862

CAMPHOR AND FLOWERS. Two or three lumps of a saturated solution of camphor and alcohol, put into half an ounce of soft water, form a mixture which will revive flowers that have begun to droop and give them freshness for a long time. Let the fair ladies, whose most appropriate sphere is among the flowers, try the experiment.—*Field and Fireside*, April 11, 1865

"GARDENING" FOR LADIES. Make up your beds early in the morning, sew buttons on your husbands' shirts; do not rake up any grievances; protect the young and tender branches of your family; plant a smile of good temper in your face; and carefully root out all angry feelings, and expect a good crop of happiness.—*Southern Cultivator*, May–June 1863

WOMEN. There are four things that look very awkward in a woman, viz: To see her undertake to whistle, throw a stone at a hog, smoke a cigar, and climb over a garden fence.—*Southern Cultivator*, July 1861

TO GET A TIGHT RING OFF A FINGER. Thread a needle, flat in the eye, with a strong thread; pass the head of the needle, with care, under the ring, and pull the thread through a few inches toward the hand; wrap the long end of the thread tightly around the finger, regularly down to the nail, to reduce its size. Then lay hold of the short end and unwind it. The thread passing through the ring will gradually remove it from the finger. This method never fails.—*Confederate States Almanac*, 1865

VERMIN RIDDANCE. Half an ounce of soap boiled in a pint of water, and put on with a brush while boiling hot, infallibly destroys bugs and their eggs. Flies are driven out of a room by hanging up a bunch of plantain or fleawort plant, after it has been dipped in milk. Rats and mice speedily disappear by mixing equal quantities of strong cheese and powdered squills. They devour the mixture with greediness, while it is innocent to man. When it is remembered how many persons have lost their lives by swallowing mixtures of strychnine, etc., it becomes a matter of humanity to publish these items.—*Southern Watchman*, July 6, 1864

MOTHS. Wide-mouthed bottles, partly filled with molasses and water, and hung up in a garden, make excellent traps for moths, which are the parents of many destructive worms.—*Field and Fireside*, February 7, 1863

INSECT TRAPS. Scoop out the inside of a turnip. Scollop the edge of the shell and place downward in the earth. The insects will crowd under it, and the beds of the garden may soon be cleared of them.—*Field and Fireside*, February 6, 1864

PRESERVING WOOLENS. The leaves of the China tree, if plentifully strewn among woolen garments when packed away for the summer, are a complete defense against moths. They are also the very best preventive of worms in dried fruit.—*Southern Watchman*, September 17, 1862

ELDER. Cut out the following and paste it in your scrapbook. It is worth a year's subscription to any reader of this paper. The leaves of the elder, if strewn among corn or other grain, when it is put in the bin, will effectually preserve it from the ravages of the weevil. The juice will also kill bugs and maggots. Insects will never touch elder bushes. The leaves of elder scattered among cabbages, cucumbers, squash, and other plants subject to the ravages of insects, effectually shields them. The plum and other fruits may be saved by placing on the branches and among them bunches of elder leaves.—*Camden Daily Journal*, October 27, 1864

TO DESTROY WEEVILS IN RICE. As the question of food is all important now, the following plan for killing weevils and preventing their hatching in rice I have found efficacious. Put the rice in a moderately tight room and burn about ten pounds of brimstone in a large iron pot. This will kill every weevil without injuring the rice.—*Charleston Tri-Weekly Courier*, July 31, 1862

OBNOXIOUS BED-BUGS AND FLIES. Coal oil is said to be a sure destroyer of bed-bugs. Apply plentifully with a small brush or feather to the places where they most do congregate. The cure is effectual and permanent. Gilt frames and chandeliers rubbed lightly over with coal oil will not be disturbed by flies.—*Field and Fireside*, March 7, 1863

BUGS AND ROACHES. The plant commonly called "water pepper" or "smart weed," which may be found in abundance along ditches, roads, lanes, and barnyards, is an effectual and certain destroyer of the bed-bug. A strong decoction is made of the herb and the places invested with the insect washed thoroughly with it. The plant may also, with much advantage, be stuffed in the cracks and corners of the room. Elderberry leaves, laid upon the shelves of a safe or cupboard, will drive away roaches and ants, while the common house fly will not venture within smelling distance of them.—*Edgefield Advertiser*, April 27, 1864

TO KILL COCKROACHES. Mix equal quantities of red lead and Indian meal with molasses, making it about the consistency of paste. It is known to be a certain exterminator of roaches. A friend who was troubled with thousands of them rid his house of them in a few nights with this mixture. Put it upon iron plates, set it where the vermin are thickest, and they will soon help themselves, without further invitation. Be careful not to have articles of food near where you set the mixture.—*Farmer and Planter*, June 1861

TO GET RID OF COCKROACHES. Take a dish of live coals, cover with tobacco leaves, place in the closet, cupboard, or buttery, and they are no longer to be seen.—*Field and Fireside*, March 21, 1863

TO KILL ROACHES. Borax powder sprinkled about the kitchen, closets, pantries, sinks, drawers, &c., within the course of a few days, almost certainly will exterminate roaches. Unlike most other remedies, it is perfectly harmless in case it should come in contact with food.—*Field and Fireside*, August 22, 1863

ANTS. These animals are known to avoid drawers and boxes made of red cedar. Red cedar shavings placed in them, or on shelves, will repel them.—*Farmer and Planter*, March 1861

A CURE FOR RED ANTS. Common salt is a complete barrier to the approach of the red ant. Let the salt be placed so that they cannot approach the place from which you wish to repel them, without passing over it, and the remedy is complete.—*Confederate States Almanac*, 1864

ANTS. Camphor sprinkled where the ants "most do congregate" is said to prove effective for their expulsion.—*Field and Fireside*, June 6, 1863

A FACT WORTH KNOWING. "Fly time" is fast approaching, and those troublesome little insects will soon make their appearance in such numbers as to annoy housekeepers almost out of their wits. Repelling invasion seems to be the watchword, and while the gallant men of the South are up in arms to drive out the increasing hordes of the North that threaten to sweep down upon us, let not our gentle housewives forget to arm themselves against this equally pestiferous invader of their homes. Fortunately the weapons in this case are more simple, though equally as successful as cannon and rifles. Take three or four onions and boil them well in a pint of water, and then brush the liquid over your glasses and frames, and the flies will not light in smelling distance of them. The recipe is a safe one and will do no injury to your furniture.—*Keowee Courier*, May 11, 1861

TO KILL FLIES. One egg well beaten, three tablespoonfuls of black pepper ground, a sufficiency of bonny-clabber to make up an ordinary batter of cakes. Sweeten well with sugar or molasses. To be served up on shallow plates—the flies will partake freely, and soon be on the floor.—*Field and Fireside*, January 31, 1863

HOW TO GET RID OF MOSQUITOES AT NIGHT. Just put a couple of generous pieces of beef on plates near your bed at night, and you will sleep untroubled by these pests. In the morning you will find them full and stupid with beef blood, and the meat sucked dry as a cork.—*Field and Fireside*, July 11, 1863

TO DESTROY RATS. Take a handful of pumpkin seeds fresh from the pumpkin, or they may be soaked in water for a short time, and sprinkle upon them a little arsenic. Then spread them upon a piece of board and set them near a rat hole at night. In the morning both the pumpkin seeds and the rats will be missing.—*Farmer and Planter*, April 1861

ABOUT RATS. Dissolve a pennyweight of phosphorus in one-fourth of a gill of olive oil, which may be done by applying a gentle heat, and whatever substance is smeared with this compound will appear luminous for several hours. It is said that if a live rat be coated with this luminous oil, and then set at liberty, all the rats in the vicinity will immediately absquatulate to parts unknown, and never return. Also, corks cut as thin as sixpences, roasted or stewed in grease, and placed in their tracks, and dried sponges in small pieces, fried or dipped in honey, with a little oil of rhodium, or birdlime, laid in their haunts will stick to their fur and cause their departure.
—*Southern Watchman,* April 26, 1865

Remedies, Cures &
Personal Hygienics

ADHESIVE PLASTER. Take of yellow resin, half a pound; lead plaster, three pounds. Melt the lead plaster by a gentle heat, then add the resin in powder and mix. This is the plaster commonly applied to retain together the lips of recent wounds.—*Southern Confederacy*, March 12, 1861

ANTISEPTIC POWDER. To correct the offensive odor of wounds, mix one hundred parts of calcined plaster of Paris with two parts of coal tar. Rub well together. Sprinkle this upon the wound once or twice daily. They have been fully tested for years at Bellevue Hospital.—*Southern Confederacy*, July 20, 1862

TO RETAIN BEAUTY AND YOUTHFULNESS. Beauty is but the outward sign or symbol of health—health of body, brain, and heart. The bad habits and false conditions which destroy the latter render the former impossible. If you would retain your beauty, have a care of your digestion and your temper, and do not allow your intellect to lie dormant. Youthfulness of form and features depends upon youthfulness of feeling.

Spring still makes spring in the mind,
When sixty years are told—
Love wakes anew the throbbing heart
And we are never old.

If, then, you would retain youthful looks, you must do nothing that will make you feel old.—*Southern Cultivator*, January 1861

A STYPTIC TO STOP BLEEDING. Scrape fine two drachms of Castile soap and dissolve in two ounces of brandy or other common spirits. Mix well with one drachm of potash and keep in a close phial. When applied, warm and dip in pledgets of lint, and the blood will suddenly coagulate some distance within the vessel. For deep wounds and amputated limbs, repeated applications may be necessary.

BLEEDING OF THE NOSE. Bathe the nose in vinegar.—*Field and Fireside*, January 25, 1863

TO STOP BLEEDING. Bleeding from a wound on man or beast may be stopped by a mixture of wheat flour and common salt, in equal parts, bound on with a cloth. If the bleeding be profuse, use a large quantity, say about two or three pints. It may be left on for hours, or even days, if necessary. In this manner, the life of a horse bleeding from a wounded artery was saved. The bleeding ceased in five minutes after the application.—*Southern Cultivator*, September 1861

BOILS. The skin of a boiled egg, applied to a boil, will draw off the matter and relieve the soreness in a few hours.—*Tri-Weekly News*, April 5, 1865

BREATH TAINTED WITH ONIONS. Leaves of parsley, eaten with vinegar, will prevent the disagreeable consequences of eating onions.—*Edgefield Advertiser*, August 28, 1861

A REMEDY FOR BRONCHITIS. Having seen it stated that dry mullein leaves smoked in a common pipe would cure bronchitis, my wife concluded to test the matter, and after a few month's use she thinks she is cured. So writes a correspondent.—*Field and Fireside*, February 7, 1863

FOR BRUISES, SWELLINGS, SORES, &c. Take one ounce gum camphor, eight ounces gum myrrh, two more ounces cayenne pepper, and two pints of brandy, whiskey, or alcohol. After pulverizing the solid articles, put all, with the brandy or alcohol, in a stone jug. Set the jug in a kettle of boiling water and let it remain there, unstopped, about thirty minutes. Then add three tablespoonfuls of turpentine and a small amount of sweet oil. It will then be ready for use. Bathe the parts affected from ten to twenty minutes, according to the severity of the case, before a fire. Then wet a flannel with the mixture and apply it to the affected part. Repeat the application every twelve or twenty hours until well.—*Edgefield Advertiser*, June 10, 1863

AN EXCELLENT LINIMENT. Take the whites of two eggs, beaten to a froth, a wine glass each of vinegar, spirits of turpentine, and alcohol, beating it all the time. This liniment must be put together in the order mentioned or it will not be thoroughly incorporated. It is superior in all cases of sprains, bruises, &c. on man or beast.—*Field and Fireside*, March 14, 1863

BURNS, SCALDS, AND CHILBLAINS. Apply strong alum water. Keep it prepared in a bottle. Apply by wetting a cloth compress and renew it until the inflammation is removed.—*Field and Fireside*, January 25, 1863

FOR BURNS AND SCALDS. Take equal parts of olive oil and limewater, which when well mixed, form a white ointment which may be spread with a feather upon that part affected, and a thin linen rag laid over it. Two or three dressings will generally take out all the fire; after which, apply a little healing ointment. Families ought always to have this remedy by them, that it may be applied immediately after the accident. Another dressing for burns, furnished by a skillful physician, is a simple application of castor oil. Saturate lint or cotton batting with the castor oil and lay on the part affected; it will be found efficacious, if renewed frequently.—*Southern Cultivator*, March–April 1863

CURE FOR CANCER. Boil fine turkey figs in new milk, which they will thicken, when they are tender, split and apply them as warm as they can be borne to the part affected, whether broken or not. The part must be washed every time the poultice is changed, with some of the milk. Use a fresh poultice night and morning, and at least once during the day, and drink a quarter of a pint of the milk the figs are boiled in twice in the twenty-four hours. If the stomach will bear it, this must be persevered in for three or four months at least. A man aged 105 years was cured about six years before his death with only six pounds of figs. . . . A woman cured by this remedy had been afflicted ten years . . . ten pounds cured her.—*Gate City Guardian*, February 11, 1861

CURE FOR CANCER. Put the juice of sheep sorrel in a pewter plate and expose it to the sun until it becomes the consistency of a salve. Apply to the cancer and repeat applications until the latter falls out with all its fibres. Severe pain accompanies the operation, but the cure is certain.—*Field and Fireside*, July 19, 1862

CURE FOR CANCER. Take the narrow-leaved dock-root, boil in soft water, and wash the ulcer with the strong decoction, as warm as it can be borne. Fill the cavity with the liquor for two minutes. Then scrape the hulk of the root, bruise it fine, put it in gauze, and lay it over every part of the ulcer. Dip a linen cloth in the decoction and put it over the gauze. Repeat this three times in twenty-four hours, and at each time let the patient take a wine glass of the tea made of the root, with one-third of a glass of port wine sweetened with honey.—*Field and Fireside*, February 13, 1864

CASTOR OIL. Very few persons have any idea of the large yield of this oil from the bean, known amongst us as the *Palma Christi*. It grows about our lots, yards, and hedges, and is generally considered a nuisance. Farmers often try to rid their places of it. Now we have use for it, and should cultivate it largely. Every family can use castor oil. It is one of the most common and useful articles of medicine in use. The profits from cultivating it, and making oil from the seed, are very large. The oil is getting scarce, and will be much scarcer, if the war continues. Before another year rolls around, it will command enormous prices. Then let every farmer in the country cultivate more or less of the seed. We annex the follow recipe for cultivating the seed and making the oil.

Strip the seeds of their husks or pods; then bruise them in mortars. Afterwards they are to be tied in linen bags and boiled in water until the oil which they contain rises to the surface. This is carefully skimmed off, strained, to free it from accidental impurities, and bottled for use. Pressed castor oil is obtained like almond oil, by bruising the seeds into paste with water and distilling the mixture, when the oil passes over.

Plant all the seeds you can find of the castor oil plant (*Ricinou Communis*). Let the seeds be planted in good sandy soil, without being manured, six feet apart each way, three seeds to a hill. Raise your crop and there will be no difficulty in directing you in how to express the oil. It is a certain and profitable crop, and the oil is essential to the sick soldier. Think of this, you who have sons and brothers in the camp.—*Southern Confederacy*, April 22, 1862

ADMINISTERING CASTOR OIL TO CHILDREN. Pour the quantity of oil prescribed into a small earthen pan over a moderate fire. Break into it an egg and stir so as to form what some cooks call a frittered egg. When it is done, a little salt or sugar, or a few drops of orange water, or some currants, should be added. The sick child will eat it eagerly and never discover the fraud.—*Southern Banner*, September 23, 1863

TO OBTAIN ROSY CHEEKS. Cultivate a flower garden. Rise early and try to discover where the roses and carnations get their bright complexions. It is a secret worth knowing. You will find the cosmetic you seek in the same place.—*Southern Cultivator*, January 1861

HOW TO CURE CHILLS. Strong hoarhound tea, well boiled and drank freely, will cure the most obstinate case of chills on record. It is easily obtained, and the remedy should be known.—*Tri-Weekly Watchman*, April 27, 1863

REMEDY FOR CHILLS. Eat a raw onion every morning before breakfast. An old friend who has tried it says this is a sure cure.—*Tri-Weekly Watchman*, September 7, 1863

CURE FOR CHILLS AND FEVER. Bruise green sage and express a wine glass half full of the juice, fill the remaining half with any kind of proof spirits. When you feel the chill coming on, drink it, lie in a warm bed several hours, or all night. This will produce profuse perspiration, which is a sure cure. Another cure: dissolve gum gauacum [guaiacum] in spirits, use freely.—*Camden Daily Journal*, September 22, 1864

A CERTAIN CURE FOR COLDS. A remedy never known to fail. Three cents worth of liquorice, two cents worth of rock candy, three cents worth of gum arabic. Put them in a quart of water, simmer them till thoroughly dissolved; then add three cents worth of paregoric and a like quantity of antimonial wine. Let it cool and sip whenever the cough is troublesome. It is pleasant, infallible, cheap, and good. It costs only fifteen cents. (Editorial comment: We notice the above in our exchanges and suppose it is either a homeopathic prescription, or that it has not been revised since the advance in the price of drugs.)—*Southern Confederacy*, November 7, 1862

REMEDY FOR COLDS. When a man begins to cough, as the result of a common cold, it is the effect of nature herself attempting the cure, which she will effect in her own time and more effectually than any man can do, if she is left alone and her instincts cherished. What are those instincts? She abhors food and craves warmth. Hence, the moment a man is satisfied he has taken cold, let him do three things: First, eat not an atom; second, go to bed and cover up in a warm room; third, drink as much cold water as he wants, or as much herb tea as he can, and in three cases out of four, he will be entirely well in thirty-six hours.—*Yorkville Enquirer*, December 7, 1864

FOR COLDS AND COUGHS. A decoction of the leaves of the pine tree sweetened, to be freely drunk warm when going to bed at night or cold during the day, is very much used as a domestic remedy for cold and coughs. The holly root chewed, and a tea made of the blade of Indian corn, also are given for colds; the latter also in intermittent fevers, it is said, with much success.—Porcher, *Resources*, 502

COUGH MIXTURE. One teaspoonful each of liquid camphor, lobelia, and laudanum mixed with two tablespoonfuls of honey or loaf sugar. Take one teaspoonful at night and morning, or when the fit of coughing is very severe.—*Field and Fireside*, January 17, 1863

CONSUMPTION. The following is said to be an effectual remedy and will in time completely eradicate the disorder. Live temperately, avoid spirituous liquors, wear flannel next to the skin, and every morning take a half pint of new milk mixed with a wine glass of the expressed juice of the green hoarhound. One who has tried it says, "Four weeks of the hoarhound and milk relieved the pains of my breast, gave me to breathe deep, long, and free, strengthened and harmonized my voice, and restored me to a better state of health than I had enjoyed for years."—*Field and Fireside*, February 13, 1864

A NEW CURE FOR CORNS. A letter from a Tybee volunteer to the *Macon Telegraph* says: "I think some of our boys have made an important discovery by bathing in the ocean, viz: the salt water has perfectly cured bad corns on their feet. They say there is no mistake that their corns have disappeared since they have been bathing once a day."—*Rome Tri-Weekly Courier*, June 13, 1861

CURE FOR WARTS AND CORNS. The bark of a willow tree, burned to ashes, mixed with strong vinegar and applied to the parts will remove all corns or excrescences on any part of the body.

HARMLESS AND SURE CURE FOR WARTS. Take five cents worth of sal-ammonia, dissolve it in a gill of soft water, and wet the warts frequently with this solution. They will disappear in the course of a week or two.—*Field and Fireside*, May 16, 1863

TO CURE SEED WARTS. Apply a little aquafortis to the tips two or three times a day for a short time.

A CURE FOR CORNS. Dip a small piece of cotton in lamp or whale oil, apply it to the corn, and wrap a bandage around it. Repeat this for six or eight days, when the corn becomes soft and is easily removed. The experiment has been tried with success.—*Field and Fireside*, January 25, 1863

TREATMENT FOR CROUP. When a child is attacked with croup or rattles, apply to the throat a bit of fat pork plentifully sprinkled with pepper. Place upon the chest, above the pit of the stomach (or too much nausea will be created) a plaster of lard and fine-cut tobacco. Then give the child a few drops of sweet oil, or a tablespoonful of lard melted with twice as much molasses. In most cases, the patient will be entirely well in a few hours.—*Field and Fireside*, March 7, 1863

SIMPLE CURE FOR CROUP. If a child is taken with croup, apply cold water—ice water, if possible—suddenly and freely to the neck and chest with a sponge. The breathing will instantly be relieved. Soon as possible, let the sufferer drink as much as he can, then wipe dry, cover up, and soon a quiet slumber will relieve the patient's anxiety, and lead the heart in thankfulness to the Power which has given to the pure gushing fountain such medical qualities.—*Field and Fireside*, June 20, 1863

CURE FOR DEAFNESS. Sulphuric ether poured into the ear in daily doses of four to eight drops, has recently been declared by the medical faculty of Paris, a certain cure for deafness. Applications may be continued a long time, if necessary. The cure has not failed in any of the numerous cases in which it has been applied.—*Farmer and Planter*, April 1861

THE PREVAILING DISEASE. The following are said to be the most effectual remedies for the cure of diarrhea: 1. Rice, toasted till black, then to be cooked with milk or water, seasoned with salt and sugar and nutmeg, and eaten one teacupful at a time. 2. The best powdered rhubarb, to be toasted till dark brown or black, then finely pulverized. Take five to ten grains, rubbed up first with a little water, two or three times a day. Very often a single dose is sufficient.—*Edgefield Advertiser*, September 25, 1861

TOMATOES FOR CHILDREN. There is no better remedy for the derangement of the bowels in children while teething than stewed tomatoes, fed to them plentifully, care being taken to keep the child's extremities warm. Be careful to cover its neck and arms, especially of an evening; give it crushed ice to assuage thirst, if possible, rather than water; avoid cordials as they only produce fever. The tomato ought to be ripe and fresh, though the vegetables preserved in cans have been used with great success.—*Southern Federal Union*, August 18, 1861

CURE FOR DIARRHEA. According to the *Rome (Ga.) Courier*, it seems not to be generally known that the free use of ripe peaches is a prompt and certain cure for diarrhea. This writer has known cases of several months standing, which had resisted all ordinary remedies, to yield in a few days under unrestrained use of this fruit. At this season, when the disease and the remedy are both so common, the knowledge of this fact, for the truth of which the writer vouches, may save much suffering. If hospital patients suffering from diarrhea were treated freely with ripe peaches, instead of opium, the result would be greatly to the advantage of all concerned. The remedy is peculiarly valuable in the case of children. Let those who are dosing their children with drugs at this season try this pleasant remedy, and they will need no other.—*Camden Confederate*, August 2, 1862

SUMMER COMPLAINT. A few leaves of the bene plant when green, plunged a few times in a tumbler of water, makes it like a thin jelly, without taste or color, which children afflicted with the summer complaint will drink freely. It is said to be the best remedy ever discovered.—*Field and Fireside*, March 21, 1863

REMEDY FOR DIPHTHERIA. Take a handful of alder root, the same quantity of dogwood root, and the same quantity of the bark of the persimmon root. Boil them with a pint of vinegar down to half a pint, then add a very little water, a small lump of alum, and a little honey, and use as a gargle.—*Tri-Weekly Watchman*, October 10, 1862

CURE FOR DIPHTHERIA. After bathing the feet, wrap up in a warm bed, take a teaspoonful of a tincture of lobelia, and apply a tar poultice to the throat as warm as can be borne. It will afford relief in a short time.—*Yorkville Enquirer*, November 19, 1862

CURE FOR DIPHTHERIA. Inside bark of green persimmon tree, sage (say a handful of each), cayenne or red pepper, alum, table salt, the whole sweetened with honey. Boil all together and strain through a cloth. It is fit for use. Gargle the throat and swallow a small portion. It is said that hundreds of cases of this disease have been cured by this simple remedy.—*Field and Fireside*, December 3, 1864

JERUSALEM ARTICHOKE. Great use is made of this plant on the plantations of South Carolina as a tonic and diuretic for dropsy. The leaves are steeped in rum, of which a wine-glassful is administered three times a day. Among the negroes I have frequently seen it prescribed with advantage in this way. It is employed also in jaundice, the expressed juice or the infusion being used; of the former two or three spoonfuls may be given; large doses purge.—Porcher, *Resources*, 428

CURE FOR DRUNKENNESS. Sulphate of iron, five grains; magnesia, ten grains; peppermint water, eleven drachms; spirit of nutmeg, one drachm. Mix well and take twice a day. This preparation acts as a tonic and stimulant, and so partially supplies the place of the accustomed liquors and prevents that absolute physical and moral prostration that follows a sudden breaking off of the use of stimulating drinks.—*Southern Enterprise,* June 19, 1861

ANTIDOTE FOR DRUNKENNESS—FOR THE BENEFIT OF OFFIC-ERS. One strong cup of coffee without milk or sugar, and twenty drops of laudanum. Repeat the dose if necessary. Or take one teaspoonful of tincture of lobelia in a tumbler of milk; if taken every ten or fifteen minutes, it will act as an emetic; taken in longer intervals, say thirty minutes, it will act as an antidote. The Yankees declared that poisoned liquor was put on the counters in New Bern [North Carolina] to poison their soldiers. Nobody doubts liquor being poisoned, but it was made of poisons to sell to our own Southern boys; and it is horrifying to think of the liquors now being made down in cellars, of sulphuric acid, strychnine, buckeye, tobacco leaves, coloring matter, and rain water. For this poisoned liquor, the best antidote is an emetic, say lobelia and warm salt and water, and then drink freely of sugared vinegar water.—*Southern Watchman,* June 18, 1862

THE WHISKEY ERYSIPELAS. According to the *Richmond Enquirer,* a new and dreadful disease has appeared in that city. The scarcity of liquor of all kinds has started up as an arrant a race of rogues as ever breathed. They doctor whiskey. They make whiskey out of apple brandy and French brandy out of whiskey, all sorts of brandies and wines out of ingenious concoctions of all three. The whiskey—that is to say, the most of it, is not composed of but about thirty per cent of genuine alcohol, and the rest is made up of water, vitriol, and coloring matter. An old and mellow taste is secured by adding the raw flesh of wild game, or young veal, or lamb, which, after soaking for three of four weeks, imparts to the liquor a rich, soft taste. The other liquors are done up in a similar way. This stuff, if drank to excess, brings on erysipelas and other diseases of the skin and flesh and will result in death. There is comparatively little good liquor of any kind in town.—*Camden Confederate,* November 27, 1863

WATER PEPPER OR SMART WEED TEA. A writer from Manchester, S.C., recommends for our sick soldiers in camp the use of this plant in dysentery, thus: Draw a tea strong enough to taste peppery and use, instead of water, with or without sugar, hot or cold, as the patient may prefer. It may be drunk freely, having no unpleasant effect. It may be gathered and dried in the shade or used fresh. Some years ago, when that disease raged in the village where I live, I used *it only* in my household, every case recovering with scarcely impaired strength. The tea, being astringent, keeps up the strength.—Porcher, *Resources,* 371

DYSPEPSIA—TWO INFALLIBLE REMEDIES. One ounce Virginia snake root, one pint molasses, one pint cognac brandy, best. Put in a pot and boil slowly for twenty minutes. Strain, cool, bottle, and cork light. Take one teaspoonful every morning on an empty stomach. If it operates too much, take less; if not enough, take more. Take it regularly. If you use tobacco, quit at once. Or, take four sarsaparilla, bruised, and one ounce of senna and quassia. Put into two quarts of whiskey and set in the sun for three days. Shake occasionally and take three drams a day, just before eating.—*Field and Fireside*, April 18, 1863

INDIAN CURE FOR EARACHE. Take a piece of the lean of mutton, about the size of a large walnut, put it into the fire and burn it some time, till it becomes reduced almost to a cinder, then put into a clean rag and squeeze it until some moisture is expressed, which must be dropped into the ear as hot as the patient can bear.—*Edgefield Advertiser*, April 17, 1861

EARACHE CURED. Take a small piece of cotton batting or cotton wool, make a depression in the centre with the end of the finger, and fill it with as much ground pepper as will rest on a five-cent piece. Gather it into a ball, tie up, dip the ball into sweet oil, and insert into the ear, using a bandage or cap to retain it in its place. Almost instant relief will be experienced, and the application is so gentle that an infant will not be injured by it, but experience relief as well as adults.—*Edgefield Advertiser*, May 7, 1862

EPSOM SALTS. Editors, *Courier:* The process of making epsom salts is to take the bittern which is left from boiling of salt and put it into a tight vessel, and let it stand twelve to fourteen hours, and the salt will collect in the bittern, then run off all the bittern, take a spoon and scrape off the salts from the sediment of salt in the bottom of the vessel; put the salts into a vessel, bore several holes with a gimlet in the bottom of the vessel, and let it drip. It is then fit for use. The making of epsom salts should be in cold weather. In trying the above process, if you should fail, try it again, as you will be sure of success. I have used salts of my own making for the last twelve months and find it equally as good as any salts I have ever used. MARTIN JAQUES. —*Charleston Daily Courier*, January 16, 1865

ERYSIPELAS. In ninety-nine cases out of one hundred, cranberries applied as a poultice will effectually cure the erysipelas. There is not an instance known where it has failed to effect a cure if faithfully applied before the sufferer was in a dying state. Two or three applications generally do the work.— *Field and Fireside*, April 18, 1863

FOR WEAK EYES. Put two grains of acetate of zinc in two ounces of rose water. Filter the liquor carefully and wash the eyes night and morning.— *Field and Fireside*, March 28, 1863

CURE FOR FROSTED FEET. It is said that frozen feet can be speedily and certainly cured by being bathed and well rubbed with kerosene or coal oil, for a few times, at night before retiring to bed. Several persons have already tried it, all of whom unite in pronouncing it an effectual cure, which, if they are correct, is an easy and cheap mode of getting rid of a very sore and unwholesome affliction. Those who have tried it inform us that the feet should be well warmed by a hot stove during and after the application of the oil, and it will certainly effect a speedy cure. Persons suffering from the pain of frosted feet will no doubt do well in giving it a trial, for it is surely a very cheap ointment, and one which is very easily applied.—*Laurensville Herald*, April 19, 1861

HOW TO CLOTHE THE FEET AND KEEP THEM COMFORTABLE. 1. Blistering, burning, soreness, and tenderness of the soles of the feet may almost invariably be prevented, even for days together and over a heated road, by soaping the sole of the stocking—that is, covering it with a thin coating of the cheapest brown soap. This, at the same time, keeps the skin of the sole cool, hardens it, and prevents inflammation. Coarse cotton socks are the best for walking. 2. Don't wear woolen socks when marching, not even thin ones, no matter what the climate. 3. The boot or shoe should have a thick sole; it is not sufficient that they should be simply "double soled." The soles should be at least half an inch thick, if three-fourths of an inch or an inch, all the better. They are more expensive, but if well made they last a long time, and even in the warmest weather will be found easy to walk in, the feet easily becoming accustomed to their weight.—*Southern Confederacy*, May 14, 1861

SIMPLE SALVE FOR SOLDIERS' FEET. Take equal parts gum camphor, olive oil, and pure beeswax. Mix warm until they are united and become a salve. At night, wash the feet well, dry them, apply the salve, put on clean stockings, and sleep with them on. The next day, the feet will be in excellent trim for marching.—*Edgefield Advertiser*, September 25, 1861

A SURE CURE FOR A FELON. Take a pint of common soft soap and stir in air-slacked lime till it is of the consistency of glazier's putty. Make a leather thimble and fill it with the composition. Insert the finger therein, and a cure is certain.—*Field and Fireside*, June 13, 1863

FOR CAMP FEVERS. One tablespoonful of salted pepper vinegar, slightly seasoned, and put into a cup of warm water. Drink often, from four to eight cupfuls a day, with fever or without fever. Pour a cupful more or less of the salted pepper vinegar into cold water and keep the body, particularly the stomach and head, well bathed with a cloth dipped in it. Give enemas of cold water, and for oil use a tablespoonful of molasses, a teaspoonful of lard, and a teaspoonful of pepper vinegar, melted together and taken warm. If the pepper is too exciting for delicate patients, leave it out in drinks and bathings and use simply the salt and vinegar in water, and very little salt.—*Southern Watchman*, June 18, 1862

THE CONFEDERATE HOUSEWIFE

CURE FOR FITS

For a Fit of Passion—Walk outside into the open air; you may speak your mind to the winds without hurting anyone or proclaiming yourself a simpleton.

For a Fit of Idleness—Count the ticking of the clock. Do this for one hour, and you will be glad to pull off your coat the next day and work like a man.

For a Fit of Extravagance and Folly—Go to the workhouse and speak with the inmates of a jail, and you will be convinced:

> Who makes his bed of briar and thorn
> Must be content to lie forlorn.

For a Fit of Ambition—Go into the churchyard and read the gravestones; they will tell you the end of ambition. The grave will soon be your bedchamber, the earth your pillow, corruption your father, and the worm your mother and sister.

For a Fit of Despondency—Look for the good things which God has given you in this world, and to those which He has promised to His followers in the next. He who goes into his garden to look for flowers may return to the house with one blooming in this bosom.

For a Fit of Doubt, Perplexity, and Fear—Whether they respect the body or the mind—whether they are a load to the shoulders or the head, or the heart—the following is a radical cure, which may be relied on, for I had it from the Great Physician: "Cast they burden on the Lord, and *He* will sustain thee."

For a Fit of Repining—Look about for the halt and the blind, and visit the bedridden, and the afflicted and the deranged, and they will make you ashamed of complaining of your lighter afflictions.—*Southern Banner,* February 8, 1865

FRECKLES. To disperse them, take one ounce of lemon juice, a quarter of a drachm of powdered borax, and half a drachm of sugar. Mix them well and let stand a few days in a glass bottle till the liquor is fit for use; then rub it on the hands and face occasionally.—*Southern Confederacy,* March 21, 1861

TO ENCOURAGE THE GROWTH OF HAIR AND PREVENT ITS TURNING GRAY. Pour boiling water on sage leaves and let them remain for some time in the oven or near a stove. Strain and apply to the roots of the hair daily. If any pomade is needed, an equal mixture of coconut and olive oils, with a little perfume, is very efficacious.

TO CLEAN COMBS AND BRUSHES. To enough tepid water to cover the bristles, not the top of the brush, add a few drops of the spirits of hartshorn. Dip the brush several times, shaking out the water carefully, and the mixture will act like magic, leaving the brush only to be dried by a towel. Combs may be done in the same way without injury.—*Field and Fireside,* April 11, 1863

JOHN HAMMOND MOORE

AMERICAN SHAMPOO LIQUID. Three quarts rum, one pint spirits of wine, half ounce tincture of cantharides, half an ounce carbonate of ammonia, one ounce salt of tartar. The foregoing liquid requires to be used for some weeks in order to produce a decided effect, either in curling or preventing baldness.

WASH FOR REMOVING SCURF AND PROMOTING THE CURLING OF THE HAIR. Beat up the yolk of an egg in a pint of clear rain water. Apply it warm and afterwards wash the head with warm water.—*Field and Fireside*, February 14, 1863

CHAPPED HANDS. Take of borax two scruples and half an ounce of glycerine. Mix in three-quarters of a pint of boiling water and bathe the hands in it morning and evening.—*Field and Fireside*, January 2, 1864

CURE FOR HEADACHES. Drink a teacupful of camomile tea, or a small quantity of chalk scraped into a glass of water, or a teaspoonful of magnesia in a glass of water.—*Field and Fireside*, January 25, 1863

CURE FOR SICK HEADACHE. Two spoonfuls of finely powdered charcoal, drank in half a glass of water, will in less than fifteen minutes give relief to the sick headache, when caused, as in most cases it is, by a super-abundance of acid in the stomach.—*Tri-Weekly Watchman*, December 26, 1861

HOW TO PRESERVE THE HEALTH OF OUR SOLDIERS. Supply them with vegetables of one kind or another, all the year round. Salads, of some kind or another, should be boiled with the salt pork or beef, but if no salt meats they should be boiled in water with a little salt, until they are tender; then to be drained and chopped a little and put in a sauce pan, and fried a moment with lard; then moistened with spiced vinegar, spread between slices of bread, and served to the soldiers. Almost any kind of pot herb will make salad. The water cress and dandelion make the best and healthiest. But when neither of these nor mustard, nor turnip greens, can be had, cowslip, shepherd's purse, or even the red and white clover, will do pretty well, if seasoned with spiced vinegar. Plain vinegar is less wholesome than that which has had a little salt and alum added to it, and steeped with pepper and aromatic herbs tied up in a bag and suspended in the vinegar.—*Southern Banner*, March 1, 1863

PALPITATION OF THE HEART. When this arises from nervous irritability, take the following draught: Tincture of foxglove, ten drops; camphor julep, ten drachms; tincture of colombo, one drachm. Mix.—*Southern Confederacy*, March 12, 1861

HICCOUGH. Take a half teaspoonful of nitre in a half a glass of water.—*Field and Fireside*, May 25, 1861

CURE FOR HYDROPHOBIA. Dissolve a pint of common table salt in a

THE CONFEDERATE HOUSEWIFE

pint of boiling water. Scarify the part affected freely, then apply the salt and water with a cloth as warm as the patient can bear, repeating the same for at least an hour. The same recipe has been successfully applied for the bite of a rattlesnake.—*Field and Fireside*, January 31, 1863

INFLAMMATIONS. Chlorate of soda is an immediate and effectual cure for the sting of bees, mosquitoes, &c., for burns (where the skin is not broken), ringworms, and other inflammations.—*Field and Fireside*, February 13, 1864

CURE FOR INSECT BITES. Take equal parts of common salt and gun powder, moisten them with strong vinegar, and apply the same to the sting of a bee or wasp, or even the bite of a snake (saying nothing of gnats, &c.), and you need go no farther for a remedy.—*Southern Recorder*, January 21, 1862

FOOD FOR INVALIDS. Tie one pint of wheat flour in thick cotton cloth, plunge it in *boiling* water, and keep it *constantly* boiling for three or four hours. Then take it out, and the outer portion, which will have absorbed the water, can be removed like a rind, leaving the remainder dry. Prepare a gruel of it by pulverizing two large spoonfuls, making a thin paste, and pour it into half a pint of milk and water. Boil five minutes and flavor with salt. Sugar and nutmeg may be added, if desired. This preparation will be found to be palatable, nutritious, and in case of bowel afflictions highly beneficial.—*Laurensville Herald*, August 30, 1861

FOOD FOR WEAK STOMACHS. Beat up an egg in a bowl, and then add six tablespoonfuls of cold water, mixing the whole well together. Then add two tablespoonfuls of the farina of potatoes, to be mixed thoroughly with the liquor in the bowl. Then pour in as much boiling water as will convert the whole into jelly, and mix it well. It may be taken alone, or with the addition of a little milk and moist or best sugar, not only for breakfast, but in cases of great stomach debility, or in consumptive disorders, at other meals. The dish is light, easily digested, extremely wholesome, and nourishing. Bread or biscuit may be taken with it as the stomach gets stronger.—*Tri-Weekly News*, April 20, 1865

CAMP ITCH—A REMEDY THEREFOR. A gentleman who has had much experience in the treatment of that loathsome disease, the itch, furnishes the following recipe for its cure. For the benefit of our soldiers suffering with the camp itch, if you think it proper, you may publish the following: Mix sixty grains of oxide of potassium and two ounces of lard; and after washing the body well with warm soap suds, rub the ointment over the person three times a week. In seven or eight days, the acarus, or itch insect, will be destroyed. In this recipe, the horrible effects of the old sulphur ointment are obviated.—*Southern Confederacy*, February 26, 1863

CURE FOR LOVE. Take twelve ounces of dislike, one pound of resolution, two ounces of the powder of experience, a long sprig of time, fourteen drachms of the quiet of dishonor, and one quart of the boiling waters of consideration. Set them over a gentle fire of love, sweeten it with the sugar of forgetfulness, skim it with the spoon of melancholy, and put it into the bottom of your heart. Then cork it with a sound conscience, let it remain, and you will truly find ease and be restored to your right senses again. These things are to be had at Mr. Love-one-only, at the House of Understanding, next door to Reason, Prudent Street, in the Parish of Contentment.—*Camden Confederate*, January 24, 1862

FOR MEASLES. Put a small piece of yeast in a tumbler of warmed, sweetened water, let it draw, and drink a mouthful every fifteen or twenty minutes, and drink plentifully of cold or hot catnip, balsam, hoarhound, or alder tea, and use in place of oil or salts, one tablespoonful salted pepper vinegar, melted together and taken warm. Take once a day, if necessary—keep out of the wet and out-door air.—*Southern Watchman*, June 18, 1862

RECIPE FOR NEURALGIC AFFLICTIONS. Equal parts of sweet oil, spirits of hartshorn, turpentine, and camphor. It can be made an anodyne by adding a little laudanum.—*Field and Fireside*, April 11, 1863

RECIPE FOR PREPARING OPIUM. When the poppy heads are ripe, with a very keen knife make vertical incisions in them about sunset; let the incisions extend just through the outer skin. A cream-colored juice will exude from each incision. Scrape off the juice very early in the morning, before the sun has time to evaporate it. Put into a saucer, plate, or teacup, place in the shade, and shape while drying. The poppy heads are generally ripe from three to four days after the petals and stamens have fallen.—*Edgefield Advertiser*, June 10, 1863

LACTUGARIUM, A CHEAP SUBSTITUTE FOR OPIUM. Dr. A. H. Peck of Port Gibson, Mississippi, writes in the *Mobile Advertiser:* With a pocket knife cut the top of the lettuce off, just before or during blooming time. Scrape on a piece of glass the milk from the severed top, then apply the edge of the glass to the cut end of the plant and scrape off the milk. The exudation will now cease unless you cut water from the top of the stem, when it will pour out as before; this may be repeated with success for half a dozen times at that milking, when it ceases for that day. Repeat the process daily until the plant is exhausted of its milky fluid. The extract dries and turns brown. On the day succeeding the gathering, scrap the glass and collect the extract by pressing it into a lump, wrap in paper, and bottle tight.—*Yorkville Enquirer*, June 22, 1864

ECONOMICAL PERFUMES. Add to one pint of alcohol any of the following: (1) ounce of oil of bergamot; (2) ounce of oil or essence of sandalwood; (3) half an ounce of oil of French lavender, half an ounce of oil of berga-

THE CONFEDERATE HOUSEWIFE

mot, and one drachm oil of cloves; (4) quarter of an ounce of oil of lemon-grass and half an ounce oil of lemons; (5) quarter of an ounce of oil of petit grain and half an ounce of orange-peel. By adding four times as much alcohol to any of these recipes you may produce a very good Cologne water.—*Field and Fireside,* March 7, 1863

CURE FOR PILES. Stew a handful of low mallows in about three gills of milk. Strain it and mix about half the quantity of West Indian molasses with it. As warm as possible, to be applied externally.—*Edgefield Advertiser,* January 7, 1863

CURE FOR THE PILES. The *Unionville(Ala.) Herald* recommends this potion. Mix one tablespoonful of sulphur with half a pint of milk, to be taken the last thing every day, until favorable symptoms appear, and then occasionally, as the case may require. This is a cheap, a simple, but most infallible cure for that most painful and unpleasant disorder. It has been used with complete success in old and inveterate cases, where individuals had spent scores of dollars in medical advice. It is equally as useful as a preventive. It will injure none, and only requires a trial.—*Camden Daily Journal,* September 23, 1864

POISON ANTIDOTES. For oil of vitriol, or aqua fortis, give large doses of magnesia and water, or equal parts of soft soap and water. For oxalic acid, give an emetic of mustard and water, afterwards mucilages and small doses of laudanum. For opium or laudanum, give an emetic of mustard, and use constant motion, and, if possible, the stomach pump. For arsenic, doses of magnesia are useful, but freshly prepared hydrated oxide of iron is best. For insects taken in the stomach, drink a small quantity of vinegar and salt. For corrosive sublimate, give the white of eggs mixed with water until free vomiting takes place.—*McLeod Journal*

POULTICES. A good poultice may be made of crumbs of bread bodied with milk, sweet oil, or spring water. Brown sugar and soap make a good poultice or salve for a bite. Flax seed, or camomile flowers, bodied with tops of wormwood, make an excellent poultice for inflammations.—*Field and Fireside,* February 14, 1863

SUBSTITUTE FOR QUININE. Red pepper tea and table salt answer every purpose for chills. Say a tablespoonful of salt to a pint of tea, commencing hours before chill time, and drinking copiously of the beverage, never fails to keep off the chill. This I learned from an intelligent physician, who uses it among the whites and well as the blacks of his own family. Several of his neighbors have employed the same remedy with complete success.—*Yorkville Enquirer,* September 10, 1863

SUBSTITUTE FOR QUININE. Thoroughwort or boneset tea used hot, in the cold stages of malarial fever, and cold in the hot stages, is believed by many physicians of South Carolina, who used it since the beginning of the war, to be the very best of our indigenous antiperiodics as a substitute for quinine. It is thought to be superior in this respect to either poplar bark, willow, or dogwood. It is also an excellent stimulating diaphoretic in low fevers.—Porcher, *Resources*, 412

RHEUMATISM. Encase the affected limb in flannel thickly sprinkled with precipitate of sulphur. Apply a bandage over this and cover with oil silk or gutta-percha, which has the effect of increasing the warmth, confining the vapor of the sulphur, and also obviating the odor.—*Field and Fireside*, March 14, 1861

CURE FOR RHEUMATISM. Bathe the parts afflicted in the water in which potatoes in their skins on have been boiled, as hot as can be borne, just before going to bed. By the next morning, the pain will be much relieved, if not removed. One application of this simple remedy has cured the most obstinate rheumatic pains.—*Gate City Guardian*, February 14, 1861

CURE FOR INFLAMMATORY RHEUMATISM. Put half an ounce of pulverized saltpetre in half a pint of sweet oil. Bathe parts affected, and a sound cure will be speedily effected.—*Farmer and Planter*, February 1861

RINGWORM. Rub mercurial ointment on at night and repeat as often as necessary.

CURE FOR SCARLET FEVER. As soon as the nature of the disease is ascertained, commence rubbing the patient with a piece of fat bacon, until the surface of the whole body is saturated with the grease. Take a piece of bacon with the rind on, as it is thus more convenient to handle, and rub thoroughly twice a day. It is well to slit the soft side of the bacon, as the fat will thus be enabled to run more freely. Greasing the throat and breast alone, in this manner, has proved beneficial. Avoid the use of calomel and all other violent remedies.—*Field and Fireside*, January 25, 1863

TO PREVENT SICKNESS. Have a jug of salted vinegar, seasoned with pepper, and take a mouthful just before going to bed. The salt and vinegar make a near approach to the digestive juices of the stomach, and are besides antidotes to many of the vegetable and miasmatic poisons.—*Southern Watchman*, June 18, 1862

TO SLEEP WELL. The earth is a magnet, with magnetic currents constantly playing around it. The human body is also a magnet, and when the body is placed in certain relations to the earth, these currents harmonize—when in any other position, they conflict. When one position is to be maintained for some time, a position should be chosen in which the magnetic currents of the earth and the body will not conflict. This position, as indicated by theory, and known by experiment, is to lie with the head toward the north pole. Persons who sleep with their heads in the opposite direction, or lying

THE CONFEDERATE HOUSEWIFE

crosswise, are liable to fall into various nervous disorders. When they go back to the right position, these disorders, if not deeply impressed upon the constitution, soon vanish. Sensitive persons are always more refreshed by sleep when their heads point due north. Architects, in building houses, should bear this principle in mind.—*Central Georgian*, June 12, 1861

POSITION IN SLEEPING. It is better to go to sleep on the right side, for then the stomach is very much in the position of a bottle turned upside down, and the contents are aided in passing out by gravitation. If one goes to sleep on the left side, the operation of emptying the stomach of its contents is more like drawing water from a well. After going to sleep, let the body take its own position. If you sleep on your back, especially soon after a heavy meal, the weight of the digestive organs, and that of the food, resting on the great vein of the body near the backbone, compresses it, and arrests the flow of blood, more or less. If the arrest is partial, the sleep is disturbed, and there are unpleasant dreams. If the meal has been recent and hearty, the arrest is more decided, and the various sensations, such as falling over a precipice, or the pursuit of a wild beast, or other impending danger, and the desperate efforts to get rid of it, arouses us. That sends on the stagnating blood, and we awake in a fright, or trembling, or perspiration, or feeling of exhaustion, according to the degree of stagnation, and the length or strength of the effort made to escape the danger. Eating a large, or what is called "a hearty meal," before going to bed should always be avoided; it is the frequent cause of nightmare, and sometimes the cause of sudden death.—*Carolina Spartan*, October 27, 1864

THE REMEDY FOR SLEEPLESSNESS. How to get to sleep is to many persons a matter of great importance. Nervous persons, who are troubled with wakefulness and excitability, usually have a strong tendency of blood on the brain, with cold extremities. The pressure of the blood on the brain keeps it in a stimulated or wakeful state, and the pulsations in the head are often painful. Let such arise and chafe the body and extremities with a brush or towel, or rub smartly the hand, to promote circulation, and withdraw the excessive amounts of blood from the brain, and they will fall asleep in a few moments. A cold bath, or a sponge bath and rubbing, or a good run, or a rapid walk in the open air, or going up and down stairs a few times just before retiring, will aid in equalizing circulation and promoting sleep. These rules are simple, and easy of application in castle or cabin, mansion or cottage, and may minister to the comfort of thousands, who would freely spend money for an anodyne to promote "Nature's sweetest restorer, balmy sleep."—*Laurensville Herald*, April 12, 1861

LEATHER AS A DISINFECTANT FOR SMALL POX. It is stated that the burning of old scraps of leather about premises is a certain preventive of

JOHN HAMMOND MOORE

contagion from small pox. An eminent physician states in an exchange, that in a practice of thirty years he has never known a worker in leather, either as shoemaker or tanner, to have the disease. In Castle Thunder, in Richmond, the experiment has been successfully tried—no cases have occurred since the burning commenced. We urge upon our citizens the importance of acting upon this statement. It can do no harm, and may prevent the spread of this loathsome disease.—*Tri-Weekly Watchman*, January 30, 1863

CURE FOR SMALL POX. We find in the *Selma (Ala.) Reporter* the following recipe, which is said to be a sure cure for small pox. Take one grain each of powdered foxglove (digitalis) and sulphate of zinc. Rub them together thoroughly in a mortar with five or six drops of water. This done, add four or five ounces of water and sweeten with sugar. Dose—a tablespoonful for an adult, and one or two teaspoonfuls for a child, every two or three hours until the symptoms of the disease vanish.—*Southern Cultivator*, March–April 1862

ANTIDOTE FOR RATTLESNAKE POISON. Mix together four grains of iodate of potash, two grains of corrosive sublimate, and five drachms of bromine. Keep in a glass-topped vial, well secured. Ten drops of this mixture, diluted with a tablespoon of brandy, constitutes a dose. The quantity to be repeated, if necessary, according to the exigencies of the case.—*Field and Fireside*, March 7, 1863

TURPENTINE FOR SNAKE BITES. The turpentine should be put in a bottle; and, the mouth being placed over the spot, the liquid is brought directly in contact with the wound by inverting the bottle. It should be held there until relief is obtained. A complete alleviation of pain has been known to ensue in less than a quarter of an hour.—*Field and Fireside*, August 22, 1863

STINGS. Bind on the part a thick plaster of common salt, moistened.—*Confederate States Almanac*, 1864

PAIN IN THE STOMACH, WITH COLDNESS OR WIND. Swallow five or six grains of white pepper for six or seven mornings.—*Field and Fireside*, March 28, 1863

OUR TEETH. A clean tooth never decays. The mouth is a warm place—98 degrees. Particles between the teeth soon decompose. Gums and teeth must suffer. Perfect cleanliness will preserve the teeth to old age. How shall it be secured? Use a quill pick and rinse the mouth after eating. Brush and Castile soap every morning; the brush and simple water on going to bed. Bestow this trifling care upon your precious teeth, and you will keep them and ruin the dentists. Neglect it, and you will be sorry all your lives. Children forget. Watch them. The first teeth determine the character of the second set. Give them equal care.—*Central Georgian*, August 20, 1862

WASH FOR THE TEETH. Dissolve two ounces of borax in three pints of boiling water and, before it is cold, add one teaspoonful of spirit of camphor and bottle for use. A teaspoonful of this mixture mixed with an equal quantity of tepid water and applied daily with a soft brush preserves and beautifies the teeth, arrests decay, induces a healthy action of the gums, and makes them look pearly white. The best time to wash teeth is at night before sleeping.—*McLeod Journal*

DOGWOOD. Young branches, stripped of their bark and rubbed against the teeth, render them extremely white. It is often employed by the common people of South Carolina. In our present need of astringent antiperiodics and tonics, the dogwood bark powdered will be found the best substitute for Peruvian. And the berries of the dogwood have been highly recommended— given as a remedy for fever in place of quinine. One or two given in the form of a pill.—Porcher, *Resources,* 60

TO CLEANSE THE TEETH AND IMPROVE THE BREATH. To four ounces of fresh prepared lime water, add one drachm of Peruvian bark, and wash the teeth with the water in the morning before breakfast and after supper. It will effectually destroy the tartar on the teeth and remove the offensive smell arising from those decayed.—*Field and Fireside,* January 31, 1863

PUTRID SORE THROAT—CURE. Mix one gill of strong apple vinegar, one tablespoonful of common salt, one tablespoonful of drained honey, and a half-pod of red pepper (or half a teaspoonful of ground pepper). Boil them together to a proper consistency, then pour it into half a pint of strong sage tea. In severe cases, a half teaspoonful every hour for children; one teaspoonful for an adult. As the canker decreases, decrease the frequency of the doses.— *Farmer and Planter,* July 1861

SORE THROATS—SALT AS A REMEDY. In these days, when diseases of the throat are so prevalent and in many cases so fatal, the use of common salt is recommended as an effectual remedy. We commenced by using it three times a day—morning, noon, and night. We dissolved a large tablespoonful of salt in half a tumbler full of cold water. The result has been that during the entire winter we were not only free from the usual coughs and colds to which, so far as my memory extends, we have always been subject, but the dry, hacking cough has entirely disappeared. We attribute this satisfactory result entirely to the salt gargle.—*Camden Confederate,* May 16, 1862

AN EXCELLENT GARGLE FOR SORE THROAT. Take half a pint of rose leaf tea, a wine glass of good vinegar, honey enough to sweeten it, and a very little cayenne pepper (the seeds mashed up, will answer). Mix well together and simmer in a closed vessel. Gargle the throat with a little of it at bed time, or oftener if the throat is very sore. A simple but very useful gargle is made of vinegar and salt diluted with a little water—to be used frequently.— *Field and Fireside,* January 2, 1864

INGROWN TOENAILS. The remedy is simply blue vitriol, a small quantity mixed with an equal quantity of burnt alum, pulverized and sifted through muslin. If the toe be ulcerated, first wash it with Castile soap suds, and then apply the powder two or three times a day.—*Field and Fireside*, March 21, 1863

CURE FOR TOOTHACHE. Take a piece of sheet zinc almost the size of a four-pence half penny and a piece of silver—say a quarter or a dollar. Place them together and hold them between and contiguous to the defective tooth. In a few minutes the pain will be gone as if by magic. The zinc and silver, acting as a galvanic battery, will produce on the nerves of the tooth sufficient electricity to establish a current and consequently relieve the pain.—*Edgefield Advertiser*, February 4, 1863

INFALLIBLE CURE FOR TOOTHACHE. To a tablespoonful of any kind of spirits, add the same quantity of sharp vinegar and a teaspoonful of common salt. Mix them well together and hold the liquid in the mouth so that it can enter the cavity or hollow of the tooth. It will give almost instantaneous relief, without any increase of pain.—*Camden Daily Journal*, October 29, 1864.

YEAST FOR TYPHUS FEVER. A correspondent writes to the *London Times* that yeast is a cheap and simple remedy for typhus or low fever. A tablespoonful administered in a case where life was all but extinct, repeated every ten minutes until the cure was effected, restored the patient to such perfect health that he was at his work in a few days' time. A small quantity, infused in the common drink of those who cannot obtain a sufficiency of nourishing food, might infuse such an amount of vitality in the constitution as might enable it to resist the depressing tendencies of the disease.—*Yorkville Enquirer*, April 22, 1863

WATERMELON SEEDS The seeds of watermelons are employed, to a considerable extent, as a remedy for strangury and other afflictions of the urinary passages. They are also highly esteemed by many experienced physicians as a valuable diuretic. They are given in an infusion made with one or two ounces of the bruised seeds to a pint of boiling water and taken cold *ad libitum*. As this is the season when watermelons are abundant, would it not be well for families to secure a sufficient supply of the seeds for medicinal purposes. To preserve them, dry them in the sun for two days, taking them in at night.—*Central Georgian*, September 10, 1862

TO STOP VOMITING. Drink very warm water, or apply cloths wet with warm brandy to the chest. Mustard plasters are very helpful.—*Field and Fireside*, January 25, 1863

FOR WEAKNESS OR GENERAL DEBILITY. To a pint of port or Madeira wine, put an ounce of steel filings and an ounce of cinnamon. Take three spoonfuls a day.—*Southern Recorder*, March 29, 1864

WHOOPING COUGH. The following is a certain remedy for whooping cough, always breaking it after the use of the medium for three days. Four ounces flax seed, three ounces honey, one ounce liquorice, and four ounces lemon juice. To be boiled together in half a gallon of water. To be well strained, bottled tightly, and kept in a cool place. Dose: a tablespoonful six times a day, to be given always after the coughing ceases.—*McLeod Journal*

CURE FOR WHOOPING COUGH. Dissolve one ounce of assafoetida in one pint of Jamaica rum. Mix with honey or syrup, and take a teaspoonful after each paroxysm of coughing until three or four have been taken during the day.—*Camden Confederate*, August 15, 1862

WHOOPING COUGH. Dr. Wilsell, of South Carolina, recommends the use of nitric acid diluted and sweetened so as to resemble lemonade as a palliative in whooping cough. He lets his patients drink as much as they please of it.—*Field and Fireside*, January 31, 1863

TO PREVENT WOUNDS FROM MORTIFYING. Sprinkle sugar on them. The Turks wash fresh wounds with wine and sprinkle sugar on them. Obstinate ulcers may be cured with sugar dissolved in a strong decoction of walnut leaves.—*Edgefield Advertiser*, September 5, 1861

SMOKE TO CURE WOUNDS. Smoking tag lock held under a bleeding wound prevents suppuratum and heals quickly. The smoking of wood would produce the same results. There is a principle in the smoke of wood, which, when applied to the blood coagulates the albumen, thus rendering it unsusceptible to putrification. The same principle stops bleeding by coagulating the blood and promotes healing.—*McLeod Journal*

TO REMOVE MAGGOTS FROM WOUNDS. Take the leaves, bark, flowers, or berries of the common elder, make a strong tea by pouring boiling water on them and letting them steep. Wash the wounds once or twice a day with this. Boil some lard and, while boiling, stir in elder in considerable quantity, and strain off through a sieve or coarse cloth. This makes an ointment for the same purpose. It is improved by adding one-fourth as much common beeswax as the amount of lard used.—*Yorkville Enquirer*, July 24, 1862

A VALUABLE RECIPE FOR SOLDIERS. Many a man who has bled to death upon the battlefield could have been saved by a handful of flour bound upon the wound. Many soldiers do not know that gun powder is one of the best styptics. Reduce the grain to dust, scrape a little lint from some garment, and fill it with fine powder, and apply it to the wound, binding or holding it fast. Soldiers, remember this, and you may sometimes save your own or your comrade's life.—*Southern Banner*, March 27, 1863

COTTON FOR WOUNDS. The Columbia *South Carolinian* is informed by Dr. Sill, the well-known druggist of that city, that burnt cotton is one of the best articles, next to lint, which can be applied to wounds. The latter cannot always be had; the former is abundant and easily obtained. Everyone has noticed that raw cotton, when plunged into water, is scarcely more than dampened externally; when burned or scorched and submitted to the same process, it is instantly wet through. This is owing to the destruction of the oily principle which it contains, which oil prevents the healthy use of cotton on wounds.—*Albany Patriot*, July 7, 1864

TO PRESERVE DEAD BODIES. The following preparation, which has been used on many occasions for thirty or forty years, comes highly recommended for the preservation of dead bodies. It will, in great degree, prevent the offensive odor from corpses; and, while the remains of so many of our deceased soldiers are being transported from the camps homeward, it may be of service to publish: Take two pounds of common salt, two pounds of alum, one pound of saltpetre—dissolve in six gallons of water and keep the shrouding wet with the mixture.—*Charleston Tri-Weekly Mercury*, March 22, 1862

Care of Fowls, Animals & Property

HINTS FOR THE MONTH

Prepare for the war! should be written over the door of every farm building. Save all the provender you can that will nourish man or beast. Take care of your straw, chaff, bran, every thing, and don't feed extravagantly because you have full cribs. Fix your shelters for the protection of stock during winter. Repair all farm buildings. Take care of your stock.

Don't indulge any longer in mutton, but look to the wool, and guard against hard times. Set all the old folks to knitting stockings for the soldiers. Half a pound of cotton and half a pound of wool will make four pairs of heavy winter socks, and they will be sorely needed. We have no Yankee knitting looms, and must rely upon our fingers.

Get your horses in marching order. We may need more cavalry, and every man who can spare a horse should freely offer him to his country.

Prepare early to sow a large area in wheat, rye, and barley. Sow large turnip patches. Red-top will do well sown any time in September. Save all your peas and pea vines. Pick your cotton as rapidly as it opens, and don't let a bale of it leave your gin house until the blockade is raised, and it can be made available by your Government.

Work day and night—not to make money, but to be able to protect the soldier and his family, and secure our independence.—*Farmer and Planter*, September 1861

HINTS FOR FARMERS.

Toads are the best protection of cabbage against lice. Plants, when drooping, can be revived by a few grains of camphor. Pears are generally improved by grafting on the mountain ash. Lard never spoils in dry weather, if it is cooked enough in trying out. In feeding with corn, sixty pounds ground goes as far as one hundred pounds in the kernel. Corn meal should never be ground very fine, as it injures the richness of it. Turnips of small size have double the nutritious matter that large ones have. Rats and other vermin are kept away from grain by a sprinkling of garlic when packing the sheaves. Timber, when cut in the spring and exposed to the weather with the bark on, decays much sooner than if cut in the fall. Wild onions may be destroyed by cultivating corn, ploughing, and leaving the field in its ploughed state all winter.—*Tri-Weekly News*, April 29, 1865

Mr. Editor: One of the best overseers I ever had laid down the following rules for his regulation. There are some excellent things in them, and I would advise overseers to write them down and place them over their mantelpieces for observance. P. C.

Rules

1. Before going to bed, I will think over what I have to do the next day, and note in upon my slate, in order that it may be recollected on the morrow.

2. I shall rise early, and never let the negroes catch me in bed of the morning, but see that they are all put regularly to their work.

3. After rising, I shall not idle about, but go directly to the business of my employer. I shall see that the negroes are at their work, that the horses have been fed, the cattle attended to, &c. If any of the negroes have been reported as sick, I shall, without a moment's delay, see what ails them, and if they be really sick, I shall at once see that proper medicine and attendance are given.

4. Whenever the negroes are working, I shall consider it my duty to be frequently with them in order that I might see how they get along. I shall not content myself with doing this once a day, but I shall do so repeatedly, observing every time what they are doing, and how they do it. I shall not permit them to do any work wrong, if it take them the whole day to do it right.

5. *Negroes.*—I shall see that the negroes are regularly fed, and that they keep themselves clean—once a week at least, I shall go to each of their houses, and see that they have been swept out and cleaned. I shall examine their blankets, &c. and see that they have been well aired—that their clothes have been mended—-and everything has been attended to, which conduces to their comfort and happiness.

6. *Horses.*—I shall consider it my business to see that the horses are properly fed and rubbed, that their stable is well littered. When harnessed and at work, I shall see that their harness fits and does not gall them, recollecting that these animals, though dumb, can feel as well as myself.

7. *Cattle.*—I shall daily see that the cattle have been penned and have good litter to lie upon, that they have good water to drink, and that their pasture is good. If they should happen not to have good pasture, I shall at once see how I can procure it for them. I shall let the "cattle minder" know that he is watched and held responsible for these things.

8. *Milch Cows.*—I shall contrive to procure these the best pastures—if possible. I shall feed them night and morning, and shall so manage it, as always to have something for them to eat when penned.

9. *Houses, Fences, &c.*—I shall endeavor never to let these get out of order. The moment I discover any of them out of repair, I shall have them attended to, never forgetting that "a stitch in time saves nine."

10. *Carts, Wagons, &c.*—I shall observe the same rules about them as about the houses, &c., and shall never put off attending to them until I may want to use them, because then I will not have the time to do so.

11. *Time.*—I will always recollect that my time is not my own, but my employer's, and I shall consider any negligence of his business, as so much unjustly taken out of his pocket.

12. *Visits.*—If anyone call to see me, I shall entertain him politely, but I shall not forget to attend to my business on that account. Business first and amusement afterwards shall be my motto. If any of my friends are displeased at this rule, the sooner they cease to be my friends, the better.—*Southern Recorder,* May 5, 1863

MAKE YOUR NEGROES COMFORTABLE. The African is a child of the tropics. He luxuriates in the intense heat of our summers, but is liable to serious injury from cold. Even our mild winters are hurtful to him unless he is comfortably clad and well housed. Economy, as well as humanity, requires us to supply our laborers with shoes and adequate clothing for the cold season, and to see to it that their houses are clean, dry, and capable of protecting their inmates from the cold air of our winter nights. They should be required to retire early. The efficiency of our laborers depends upon their health, and this, as with us, depends upon our avoidance of the causes of disease, prominent among which, is an undue degree of cold. In proportion as you promote their bodily comfort do you promote their health and usefulness.—*Southern Cultivator,* January 1861

VISITING AMONG SLAVES. Since the construction of numerous rail-roads through the Southern States, writes the *Madison (Ga.) Visitor,* the social privileges between slaves in distant localities have been increased far more proportionally than those of the white population. But for the gratuitous inter-ference and contaminating influence of our fanatical neighbors and visitors from Northern States, these privileges would have been still more increased, not only on account of the cheapened facililties for intercourse, but also on account of a constantly increasing confidence between master and slave, aside from this pestiferous influence.

As things now are, it has become evident to all observant members of Southern society, that a proper regard for the safety and peace of the country, as well as humanity of the slaves themselves, require that during the continu-ance of the present excitement these social privileges of slaves, so much desired by them, and so readily granted heretofore by owners, must be curtailed. In-stances, commendatory of this policy, are occurring constantly in almost every community, and yet it is a source of annoyance, all over the country, that there are persons of kind disposition who have become so accustomed to grant these indulgences, and confide in their servants, that they continue to grant these social indulgences, notwithstanding the motives and interest and safety to the country. . . . Safety, at this time, consists in most vigilant circumspection, and nothing should be tolerated that affords the semblance of an opportunity to inflict injury upon any portion of the community.—*Southern Cultivator*, May 1861.

MOLASSES INSTEAD OF BACON. The *Macon Telegraph* says: A planter in Mississippi states that seven years ago he commenced giving his negroes two pounds of bacon and two pints of molasses per week, instead of four pounds of bacon as before. His negroes soon began to like the molasses better than the meat, and he now looks to Louisiana for half the meat used on his plantation. The medical faculty of London, several years since, declared that those who live on molasses as a part of their diet never have typhoid fever. The Mississippi planter's experience corroborates this decision, for his negroes have not had a single case of typhoid fever among them, although frequently in the neighborhood and once in his own family. Let the planters of Georgia try this experiment. It will save more than one-half. So much fat bacon and grease in our climate is injurious and unhealthy. The negroes on sugar plantations are always sound and healthy.—*Albany Patriot*, June 27, 1861

COSTUME FOR NEGROES. A prolific and baneful source of the de-moralization and dishonesty of our negroes is their insane passion for *imitating* their masters and mistresses in the matter of *dress*. Like the peasantry or rural population of other countries, the costume of our negroes should be *regulated by law*, and they should never be allowed to array themselves in public in the cast-off finery of their betters. To a person of refined taste, the airs and assumptions of dandified negroes (male and female) is most disgusting and offensive; and, their desire to possess themselves of flashy and expensive clothing leads to the commission of numberless crimes and immoralities, and seriously undermines all proper subjection and discipline.—*Southern Cultivator*, March 1864

COMFORT TO BRUTES. An animal may be well fed, lodged, and prop-erly cleaned without being comfortable; and, in men as well as brutes, want of comfort operates on the digestive powers. If the surface of a stall in which an ox or horse stands deviates much from the level, he will be continually uneasy. And he will be particularly so at night, if its surface is rough, or if a proper bed of litter is not prepared every evening for it to repose on. The forms of racks and mangers is often less commodious than might be, and may become a source of uneasiness and disquiet amounting to absolute suffering. A hayrack that projects forward is bad because the animal, in drawing out the hay, is teased with the hay seeds falling into his eyes and ears. And this form, it may be added, is apt to cause the breath of the animal to ascend through its food, which must, after a time, render it nauseous. For this reason, hay should lie as

THE CONFEDERATE HOUSEWIFE

short a time as possible in lofts above the animals and, when practicable, should be fed to them direct from the rick or stack, standing outside the building in pure atmosphere.—*Field and Fireside,* January 10, 1863

CHARCOAL FOR ANIMALS. A half pint of it finely pulverized and mixed with corn, meal, and water, to each animal once or twice a week, will be found extremely beneficial in aiding digestion and prevent any derangement of the stomach arising from overfeeding, as is liable to be the case with the hoggish animal. Besides serving as a medicine, it is extremely fattening, either in itself or by rendering the food eaten more available, by correcting and stimulating the digestive powers.

Charcoal has also been known to work wonders in fattening poultry, geese, ducks, &c. It may be given in the same way as recommended for swine. Fowls that have been accidentally confined for a long time where they had access to no food, except charcoal, when discovered were found not only to have sustained themselves, but to have actually fattened.—*Field and Fireside,* February 14, 1863

CURRY COMBS. There is a small item of expense, to which we would call the attention of our readers, we think it advisable to incur every spring, but which, we fear, most of our planting readers never trouble their pockets about. It is the expense of buying a curry comb for each mule and horse on the plantation, and when bought, requiring the overseer to have one of them used while the teams are eating in the morning. In these scarce times it behooves every planter to save all he can, and we give it as our firm belief, that a mule well curried every morning will do as much work, and keep in as good working order, on eight *good* ears of corn at a meal, as one never curried will on ten of the same kind of ears at each feed. If you doubt our assertion, just invest *a quarter* in a curry comb (for a ten cent's comb is not worth taking home) and try the experiment for yourself from now till your crop is laid by.—*Farmer and Planter,* February 1861

SHELTER. There is one truth that every farmer who ever winters a herd of any kind of animals should appreciate—and that is that *"shelter is cheaper than fodder."* Exposed animals will consume a third more food and come out in the spring in worse condition. The loss of animals by death in wintering, when suffering from all the severities of piercing winds, drifting snows, and cutting sleet, is sometimes greater in two or three years than the cost of substantial and comfortable buildings for protection, and the loss of fodder consumed, in any case, would in a few years pay for their erection.—*Edgefield Advertiser,* November 5, 1862

WORTH KNOWING. An exchange declares that corn stalks, if saved, are full equal to the same weight of hay. Prepare them by cutting into pieces of half an inch in length, and place in hogsheads. Throw in one gallon of boiling water, containing one gill of salt, cover the hogsheads with a blanket—the steam swells and softens the stalk. Then add a little meal and feed it to the cattle.—*Camden Daily Journal*, November 22, 1864

FILM ON THE EYE. The easiest as well as most effectual remedy for removing a film from the eye of an animal is simply to put a teaspoonful of molasses on the eye-ball. Oxen, horses, cows, and sheep have, in this manner, been relieved.—*Confederate States Almanac*, 1864

Milk Cows Are Selling at $500.00

Yesterday I went to the village [Spartanburg]. The trip was extremely unpleasant in many respects. I intended to come home last night but was prevented by a storm. If I had been alone I would have started before the storm. I was dreadfully put out by being compelled to stay. When I reached home I found the negroes skinning two of my finest milk cows. A tree fell across the fence of Dr. Dean's cane patch, they walked in and killed themselves eating cane. No one can tell how I feel at the loss of these cows. I have had some feelings about it which I never had, about the loss of property, before. It will cause us, white and black, to sit down to many dry suppers. Times has been that if we needed a milk cow we could go and buy one. Now we cannot. We have not the means and besides, we could scarcely find the cow if we had. Milk cows are selling at $500.00.

—David Golightly Harris Journals, September 6, 1864.

This entry is by Emily Liles Harris, who continued her husband's farm diary after he went to war.

A CAT HINT. When a cat is seen to catch a chicken, tie it around her neck and [make her] wear it for two or three days. Fasten it securely, for she will make incredible efforts to get rid of it. Be firm for that time, and the cat is cured. She will never again desire to touch a bird. This is what we do with our own cats, and what we recommend to our neighbors, and when they try the experiment, they and their pets are secure from reproach and danger henceforth. Try it.—*Southern Lutheran,* October 30, 1861

HOW TO THROW AN OX. Mr. L. Henck, in the *Genesee Farmer,* thus describes a simple method practiced by him on one occasion when he wished to extract hedgehog quills from the animal's hind foot. The ox was first place on smooth ground, and the left, or near side, fore foot tied to the leg above the knee. Then a rope was tied around the ankle of both of the off side feet, and two men, standing on the near side, pulled gently on these ropes, at the same time crowding against his side. A man was stationed at the off side of the animal's neck, to attend to the head while coming down. The animal, seeming to fear a fall, readily dropped on his knees, and down on his side. The ropes were then securely held, and the quills easily extracted with a bullet-mold for nippers.—*Farmer and Planter,* February 1861

HOW TO DRIVE OXEN. The driver of an ox team should walk directly opposite the yoke, walk straight, and carry his whip as upright as his gun. Use a whip stock with a short lash, and touch the cattle only with the lash, and never strike them on the nose or above the eyes.—*Southern Recorder,* January 21, 1862

WOUNDS IN CATTLE. The most aggrieved wounds of domestic animals are easily cured with a portion of the yolk of eggs mixed in spirits of turpentine. The part affected must be bathed several times with the mixture, and a perfect cure will be effected in forty-eight hours.—*Edgefield Advertiser,* April 17, 1861

RELIEVING CHOKED CATTLE. It is said that pouring into the throat half a pint, more or less, of sweet oil (or lamp oil) will so lubricate the obstruction that rubbing the throat briskly outside with the hand will soon remove it—sliding it up and down according to its position. In any case, the oil is a useful auxiliary to other means.—*Edgefield Advertiser,* November 5, 1862

BLOATED CATTLE. For cattle in this condition, a dose of thorough-wort with a little tansey will afford immediate relief. It should be given warm. If one dose is not enough, administer another—and let the animal be driven about the yard till relieved.—*Field and Fireside,* April 11, 1863

BREAKING STEERS TO THE YOKE. The winter before they are two years old, get them into a yard and then into a small pen so strong they cannot break out. Feed them corn-nubbing [nubbin] and handle them gently.

JOHN HAMMOND MOORE

Get them yoked, if possible, before they are aware of it. Then feed them more corn. Now hitch them behind a steady yoke of cattle, drive them around awhile, feed them more corn, and make them fast. Then unyoke them and feed a little more corn. Repeat the whole operation the next day twice, morning and evening; do not forget the corn. The third day put them in the lead. Handle them a little every day, morning and evening; yoke and unyoke them every time. Do not beat them. If you cannot make them do as you wish, and get vexed with them, do not abuse them, but feed them corn. You will soon be able to drive them alone. This should be done soon, as they never will be broken right without. Now, if you have a small stock and a light sled, they will haul enough to feed them, and this will be enough for them to do morning and evening, and they will very soon be quite handy. But mind, you must give them corn every time you yoke, and enough, until they become quiet, so that you can handle them and get up to them in any place, and they never will forget it, but continue quiet and gentle all their lives.—*Edgefield Advertiser*, April 13, 1864

COVER THE YOKE. Sore necks of oxen are sometimes cured by covering the yoke with sheet lead. White lead is also an excellent thing to dry up the sores of oxen and horses, and is well worth trying.—*Edgefield Advertiser*, June 15, 1864

LIVE CATTLE WEIGHED BY MEASURE. The only instrument necessary is a measure with feet and inch marks on it. The girth of the circumference of the animal is just behind the shoulder blades. The length is the distance from the shoulder blades. The superficial feet are obtained by multiplying the girth and length. The following table contains the rule to ascertain the weight of the animal.—

If less than one foot in girth, multiply the superficial feet by eight.
If less than three and more than one, multiply the superficial feet by eleven.
If less than five and more than three, multiply the superficial feet by sixteen.
If less than seven and more than five, multiply the superficial feet by twenty-three.
If less than nine and more than seven, multiply the superficial feet by thirty-two

Example: Suppose the girth of a bullock to be six feet, three inches, length five feet, six inches, and the superficial area will then be thirty-four; and, in accordance with the preceding table, the weight will be seven hundred and eighty-two pounds.

Example: Suppose a pig to measure in girth two feet, and length one foot and nine inches. There would then be three and one-half feet, which multiplied by eleven, gives thirty-eight-and-a half pounds as the weight of the animal when dressed. In this way, the weight of the four quarters can be substantially obtained during life.—*Albany Patriot*, May 26, 1864

TO CURB JUMPERS. To prevent steers from jumping fences, clip off the eyelashes of the under lid with a pair of scissors, and the ability or disposition to jump is as effectually destroyed as Sampson's power was by the loss of his locks. The animal will not attempt a fence until the eyelashes are grown again.—*Field and Fireside*, December 3, 1864

COW HAIR—A SUBSTITUTE FOR WOOL. Whip the hair clean from dirt and lime, wash and dry it well, and mix with cotton. Spin fine or coarse as needed. It makes excellent gloves, socks, blankets, and men's clothing. Said to be warmer, heavier, and more lasting than wool. I expect to wear cow hair clothes this winter. Many ladies are doing this, but all do not know of this plan, and if the editors through the country would publish this, thousands of soldiers this winter might be warmly clad.—*Edgefield Advertiser*, January 18, 1865

CURE FOR DISTEMPER IN DOGS. To a grown dog give half a teacupful of castor oil. If that does not cure, repeat the dose the third day, which I have never known to fail in making a cure.—*Field and Fireside*, June 27, 1863

CURE FOR MANGE. Take one pint common, soft lye soap, one-half pint sugar, one-half pint powder of sulphur, and one pint of coal tar. Mix well together. A single application, well rubbed into the dog's skin (not merely daubed on the hair), will in two weeks time effect the cure. Tie the dog after the application, in the sun for two hours, until dry, with the head well up, so as to prevent rolling. Then let him go until the application gradually wears off, which will be in about two weeks. Try it.—*Edgefield Advertiser*, March 16, 1864

FEED BONE TO HENS. If you take fresh bones from the kitchen, and with a sledge, on a rock, or any natural or artificial anvil, pound them up into small pieces, hens will eat them ravenously, and not only will they digest the bones and make a better manure of them than can be made in any other way, but they will be themselves greatly benefitted by them. They will lay throughout the season with much greater regularity then otherwise, and will fatten on the marrow within, and the fat and muscle that adhere to the bones.—*Southern Cultivator*, April 1861

FOOD FOR POULTRY. Boiled beans are first-rate food for all kinds of poultry, particularly laying hens. It is well to mix meal with them, in equal quantities, in boiling water, and mash them up together.—*Edgefield Advertiser*, May 8, 1861

GAPES IN CHICKENS. May be easily cured by giving them small crumbs of dough impregnated with a little soft soap. Once or twice is sufficient.—*Edgefield Advertiser*, November 20, 1861

TO FATTEN POULTRY. Three things are necessary to perfect success. First, meat (fat back or cracklings); second, charcoal broken up small; third, gravel and water. Commence with milk well mixed with charcoal. Wheat scranings and fat pork, or fried meat as cracklings, are the best articles of food. A piece of fat pork, as large as can be thrust down the throat, is a simple and certain cure for the pip.

ADVICE FROM PETERSBURG, JULY 17, 1864

I think the copperas and sulpher [sic], ashes and salt, and corn soaked in tar water will stop the disease among your hogs. Let those that die be buried deep, deep, so they cannot be scratched up. See that the sheep have a good chance and are in fine condition to enter on the winter. For the rest, my darling wife, trust all in God. I don't believe He intends we should be too wise in our providing. We have plenty to encourage us. Make all the syrup you can, and let us keep an abundance on hand for the negroes. Continue to plant such vegetables, after rain, as do well later in the season. Save all the peas you possibly can, and if we have rain, we'll do very well. Have the colts well cared for and Brown Bess worked enough to ascertain she'll work kindly in the carriage. You know your horses may be taken at any time. The investment in mares was a good one, the best we now have. Horses are very high, and they must continue to go up.

**—Epworth Bird to his wife Sallie in Hancock County, Ga.,
in Rozier, ed., *Granite Farm Letters*, 174–75**

TO DISTINGUISH GOOD EGGS FOR SETTING. All those having setting hens would to well to take notice of the following remarks, and they will have a chicken for every egg set. Take eggs not more than three or four days old, and have a candle or lamp. Hold the egg in one hand with the broad end close to the candle. Place the edge of the other hand on top of the egg, and you will immediately perceive the incubation and some people can tell a pullet from a rooster. The mark of a rooster is crosswise and a pullet, lengthwise. Another way is to place your tongue on the large end of the egg, and you will find a strong heat if fresh and good, and less heat if old and doubtful. Eggs put up for hatching should never be put in a damp cellar, as the dampness destroys the heat.—*McLeod Journal*

TO MAKE HENS LAY PERPETUALLY. I never allow cocks to run with my hens, except when I want to raise chickens. Hens will lay eggs *perpetually*, if treated in the following manner: Keep no roosters; give the hens *fresh meat* chopped fine like sausage meat, once a day to each hen, during the winter, or from the time insects disappear in the fall, till they appear again in the spring. Never allow eggs to remain in the nest, for what are called *nest eggs*. When the roosters do not run with the hens and no nest eggs are left on the nest, the hens will not cease laying after the production of twelve or fifteen eggs, as they always do when the roosters and nest eggs are allowed, but continue laying perpetually. My hens lay in winter, and each from seventy-five to one hundred eggs in succession. There being nothing to excite the animal passion, they never attempt to set. If the above plan were generally allowed, eggs would be just as plenty [*sic*] in winter as summer. The only reason why hens do not lay in winter as freely as in summer is the want of animal food, which they get in abundance in the form of insects. The reason they stop laying and go to setting, after laying a brood of eggs, is the continual excitement of the animal passion of the males. I have for several winters reduced my theory to practice and proved its entire correctness. It must be observed the presence of the enemy is *not* necessary for the production of eggs, as they are formed whether the male be present or not. Of course, such eggs will not produce chickens. When chickens are wanted, the roosters of course must run with the hens.—*Field and Fireside*, January 18, 1862

TO DESTROY LICE ON HOGS. Take common tar and smear it on the side of trees and logs about the hog pen, of suitable height for the hogs to rub against. Every hog you have, as soon as he smells it, goes immediately to rub himself against the tar, which will destroy the lice. Care should be had in smearing the tar to put it high enough and low enough to suit the different heights of all your hogs, and to use it often enough for all to partake of it.—*Spartanburg Express*, July 3, 1861

CURE FOR HOG CHOLERA. Beat up an ounce or more of assafoetida, and add say to an ounce, a pint of whiskey or other kind of spirits, and give to the hog two tablespoonfuls. It produces an immediate relief and speedy and permanent cure. The effect which the drink has is to cause hogs to vomit the most disgusting and loathsome mass of matter conceivable from the stomach, after which an immediate reaction takes place, and the hogs are soon entirely well.—*Yorkville Enquirer,* January 6, 1864

COST OF KEEPING A HORSE. My experience has led me to believe that a horse weighing a thousand pounds, and being worked more or less several times a week, can be well kept on fifteen pounds of hay (five pounds at each meal), with three quarts of corn, or six quarts of oats, per day. The cost will, of course, vary according to the prices of hay or grain. When hay is worth, as it is now, $20 a ton at the barn, and oats 50 cents per bushel, the cost would be about $1.70 a week. Many owners of horses, especially farmers, are apt to give their horses too much hay. It is not necessary that the feeding rack should be kept full of hay all the time; this is decidedly injurious to their health and usefulness. If hay is cut, they can consume enough in six hours out of the twenty-four, two at each meal, to keep them in good condition, and they will be less liable to contract diseases, especially heaves, than if more is fed to them.—*Southern Cultivator,* October 1861

SLABBERS IN HORSES. Green burdock leaves will cure the slabbers in a horse in fifteen minutes, if he will eat them, and usually a horse troubled in that way will eat them.—*Farmer and Planter,* February 1861

TO PREVENT HORSES BEING TEASED BY FLIES. Take two or three small handfuls of walnut leaves, upon which pour two or three quarts of cold water. Let it infuse one night, and pour the whole, next morning, into a kettle, and let it boil for a quarter of an hour; when cold, it will be fit for use. No more is required than to moisten a sponge and, before the horse goes out of the stable, let those parts which are most irritable be smeared over with the liquor, viz: Between and above the ears, the neck, the flank, &c. Not only the lady or gentleman who rides out for pleasure will derive benefit from this preparation, but the coachman, the wagoner, and all others who use horses during the hot months.—*Edgefield Advertiser,* April 17, 1861

HORSE LAMENESS—HOW DISCOVERED. Take notice, that in examining a horse for lameness, you may often detect it by only looking at his ears; for all horses that are lame before, drop their heads when they throw their weight onto the sound leg; and those that are lame behind, throw their heads up when the sound leg comes to the ground.—*Southern Cultivator,* July 1861

TO CURE INFLUENZA IN HORSES. Mix a tincture of iron in two drachm doses in oatmeal or corn meal gruel with a little brandy, wine, or good rye whiskey, say about three ounces to a quart of gruel, to be given twice a day; any mucilaginous drinks would be proper at any time of the day.—*Southern Federal Union*, July 16, 1861

HEAVES IN HORSES. Well cured corn stalks, cut before frost, are the best fodder for horses that have the heaves. Cases taken in time have been ultimately cured by constantly feeding on them. Hay, cut fine, and wet before feeding, will greatly alleviate all symptoms of heaves; and, even in old and incurable cases, the disease will often be *suspended* while horses are thus fed.—*Edgefield Advertiser*, November 5, 1862

HINTS FOR FARMERS AND MILLERS. Careful observation for many years establishes the fact that a horse fed on ground grain will last and work a quarter longer than he will if fed on unground corn, oats, and other whole grain. The first named will be as young and as serviceable when sixteen years old as the latter will be at twelve. Not only the grinding teeth of a horse wear out prematurely by this excess of jaw work in grinding hard corn, but the mill often barely cracks the kernels, and only the moiety of the nourishment in the grain is extracted in its passage through the alimentary canal. While the muscular labor of grinding so much grain in the lifetime of a horse is considerable, the loss in food consumed is far greater than the market value of the animal, by its not being fully digested. The loss of feeding unground corn to oxen, cows, and hogs is generally more than in feeding horses.—*Yorkville Enquirer*, April 3, 1862

TO CURE SWEENEY IN HORSES. Take a half pound of blistering ointment and a half pint of spirits of turpentine, and simmer them over a slow fire until intimately mixed—it is then ready for use, either warm or cold. Take up the skin on the shoulder of the horse, where it is diseased, between the thumb and the forefinger, and puncture it several times, through and through, with a sharp awl. Then rub it well with the preparation for three or four successive mornings, until the shoulder is blistered. When the blister heals, the horse will be well.—*Southern Recorder*, June 17, 1862

RECIPE FOR SCRATCHES IN HORSES. Take common bar lead and melt it, as you would to mould bullets. Then take flour of sulphur and sprinkle on it until the lead is entirely burnt to a powder. It must then be pounded to a fine powder and a sufficiency of hog's lard added to it to make a good ointment of proper consistence. Now trim the hair well about the diseased part, wash clean with soap and warm water, and twice a day rub this ointment on well with a corn cob. This treatment will cure the worst case of scratches or foot evil in a few days.—*Edgefield Advertiser*, September 18, 1862

CURE FOR BRITTLE HOOF IN HORSES. A mixture of one part of oil of tar and two of common fish oil, well rubbed into the crust and the hoof, will restore the natural pliancy and toughness of the horn, and very much contribute to the quickness of the growth.—*Field and Fireside*, April 11, 1863

TO TELL THE AGE OF A HORSE. After a horse is nine years old, a wrinkle comes on the eyelid, at the upper corner of the lower lid, and every year thereafter he has one well defined wrinkle for each year over nine. If, for instance, the horse has three wrinkles, he is twelve; if four, thirteen. Add the number of wrinkles to nine, and you will always get it. Our informant is confident this sign will never fail. As a good many people have horses over nine, it is easily tried. If true, the horse jockeys must give up their trade. That's a wrinkle.—*Southern Cultivator*, July–August 1863

GRUBS IN HORSES. Take one tablespoonful of alum, two new eggs, and a pint of soft soap. Put in water enough to make it thin, mix well the whole together, then make the horse drink it, and it will kill the grubs.—*Carolina Spartan*, July 21, 1864

CURE FOR WOUNDS IN HORSES. Take one gill of turpentine, two gills of whiskey, and one egg. Beat the eggs well and mix the three together. It should be applied with a feather or swab twice a day. It keeps the wound healthy and prevents it healing too rapidly.—*McLeod Journal*

FOUNDER IN HORSES. Take a tablespoonful of pulverized alum, pull the horse's tongue out of his mouth as far as possible and throw the alum down his throat, let go of his tongue, and hold up his head until he swallows. In six hours time (no matter how bad the founder), he will be fit for service.—*Yorkville Enquirer*, January 27, 1864

TO START A BALKY HORSE. Fill his mouth with dirt or gravel from the road and he'll go. Now don't laugh at this, but try it. The plain philosophy of the thing is—it gives him something else to think of. We have seen it tried a hundred times, and it has never failed.—*Yorkville Enquirer*, April 12, 1865

CANVAS HARNESS. The *Raleigh Standard* says: We saw a day or two since at the harness establishment of Col. C. W. D. Hutchings, of this place, some harness made of cloth and leather, about three-fourths of the former, which appear to be durable in their character. They were made under the direction of Quartermaster Pierce, and if they will answer the purpose—the bearings and fastenings only being of leather—a great saving in leather will be effected. They present a very neat appearance. Col. H. informs us that the savings is about twenty pounds in leather to the set.—*Southern Cultivator*, November–December 1863

STAGGERS. Sheep, as well as horses, are sometimes afflicted with the staggers. It is occasioned by improper food. Oak leaves and buds are particularly prejudicial. They bind the bowels and staggers frequently follow. To cure this disorder, dissolve half an ounce of assafoetida in two quarts of water;

give a quarter of a pint, warm, every three hours.—*Clarke's Confederate Household Almanac, 1863*

TAR FOR SHEEP. A gentleman who has a large flock of sheep says that during the season of grazing he gives his sheep tar, at the rate of a gill a day to every twenty sheep. He puts the tar in troughs, sprinkles a little fine salt on it, and the sheep consume it with eagerness. This preserves them from worms in the head, promotes their health in general, and is thought to be a good specific against the rot.—*Confederate States Almanac, 1864*

HINTS FOR GARDENERS. Never train or support a plant unnaturally. Climbers will not succeed hanging about. Trailers will do no climbing. Grow it as it would grow naturally, and supply it in such cases where nature does not. Carefully preserve fallen leaves of trees, and procure as many as you can. When rotted into mould, they are invaluable. Keep your seeds, bulbs, tubers, etc. in a place where neither heat, nor frost, nor damp can reach them, for either of these would destroy many. Do not waste rain water. Save all you can, for it is best for plants. Whenever a plant suffers a loss of root, prune off the corresponding portion of the head. Encourage toads and robins (unless you have a pet cherry tree). They gain their living by destroying insects.—*Spartanburg Express*, February 19, 1862

FEBRUARY 14, 1863—GARDEN

To day I have had the garden ploughed and such seeds planted as should have been a month ago. I have made the garden extremely rich, to make up lost time. We shall need a large garden more than usual this year. We have scarcely enough corn and meat, and no wheat. Never since we kept house has our table presented so little variety as at present. My heart grows anxious when I sit down to the table and look at the hungry mouths that are gathered around it.

—David Golightly Harris Journals

HOW TO RAISE EARLY TOMATOES. About the first of March, take a few large turnips and cut out the hearts of them to form a sort of cup. Fill the cavities with earth, and plant two or three tomato seeds in each. When the seeds have well sprouted, pull up all but the healthiest plant in each turnip, and let those that remain stand where they have the benefit of the sun; the plant will grow very thrifty—the decaying turnip furnishing it food. When the weather becomes sufficiently warm, set the turnips in well prepared soil, not less than three feet apart, make the lath frames to keep the vines from the ground, keep the soil well hilled up around them, and you will have a crop that will astonish the natives. The advantage consists in getting the plants started early without setting them back by transplanting.—*Farmer and Planter*, February 1861

SAVE YOUR SEEDS. Planters and gardeners must not rely, as heretofore, on getting their garden seeds from the Northern States. We advise them to be careful in saving a good supply of all kinds, as they will soon be ripe. Plant a large crop of Irish potatoes; they will make seed potatoes, if nothing else. Look to your interest in time.—*Tri-Weekly Watchman*, June 3, 1861

BEE ITEMS. A swarm just hived should never be placed at the side of a strong colony that has not yet swarmed, because if the weather on the next ensuing day be fine, the bees of the old stock will issue in great numbers, about noon, and disport in front of their hive. The bees of the swarm, not having yet become accustomed to their new location, will, on their return, be attracted to the busy, joyful hum of their neighbors, and tempted to join them. The loss of bees from this cause, at a time when no brood is maturing in its hive, is a very serious injury to a young swarm.—*Farmer and Planter*, June 1861

A HINT. We have found nothing so effectual in protecting the young plants of melons, cucumbers, &c. from the depredations of insects as the sowing around the edges of the hill of radish seed. The young growth of the radish is much preferred by these insects to that of the melon and cucumber; hence, while the former is freely feasted on, the latter is permitted to go scot free. If too late for trial this season, let it be remembered for the next.—*Southern Cultivator*, July 1861

IRON FOR PEACH TREES. The scales of iron that accumulate around the anvil of a blacksmith's shop are more valuable than manure for peach trees. A shovel full put around a healthy peach tree will be very likely to keep it in good condition, and it is said that trees already diseased have recovered by the application of these scales. Iron in any form will answer a good purpose.

TIMBER FOR POSTS. The best timber for posts, in order of durability, is red cedar, yellow locust, arbor vitae (or white cedar of some places), white oak, and chestnut. Charring posts of the most perishable sorts to rend them durable is of little use. The charred portions are thereby made brittle, and the only part of the post possessing strength is the interior, which is as liable to

THE CONFEDERATE HOUSEWIFE

the changes of dryness and moisture as ever through the porosity of the charcoal. Salting posts—by boring a hole obliquely downward at the surface of the earth and plugging in salt—is far more beneficial. Cases are known in this country of red cedar posts nearly a hundred years old, perfectly sound.—*Field and Fireside*, October 25, 1862

DISH WATER AND SOAP SUDS. Instead of being appropriated to the formation of an interesting puddle on the kitchen floor, they should be poured at the roots of young fruit trees, raspberry and currant bushes. This will accelerate growth and augment the size of the fruit.—*Field and Fireside*, November 5, 1862

FOND OF BONE. Place a bone in the earth near the roots of a grape, and the vine will send out a leading root directly to the bone. In its passage it will make no fibres; but, when it reaches the bone, the root will entirely cover it with the most delicate fibres, like lace, each one seeking a pore of the bone. On this bone, the vine will continue to feed as long as nutriment remains to be exhausted.—*Southern Cultivator*, March–April 1863

HOW TO DESTROY GARDEN INSECTS. A decoction of the leaves of common camomile will destroy all species of insects, and nothing contributes so much to the health of a garden as a number of camomile plants dispersed through it. No greenhouse or hothouse should ever be without it, in a green or dried state; either the stalks or the flowers will answer. It is a singular fact that if a plant is drooping and apparently dying, in nine out of ten cases it will recover if you plant camomile near it.—*Tri-Weekly Watchman*, February 27, 1863

TO CATCH CABBAGE WORMS. Break off a large leaf from the bottom of the cabbage and place it on the top, upper side down. Do this in the evening and in the morning you will find near or quite all of the worms on each cabbage have taken up their quarters on this leaf. Take off the leaf and kill them, or feed them to the chickens, and place the leaf back if there be any more to catch.—*Field and Fireside*, July 11, 1863

TO PREVENT GRUBS AND CUTWORMS. A solution or decoction made with the berries of the Pride of India tree (to a half bushel of the berries put into a barrel add fifteen gallons of water and let them soak one or two days), and sprinkled with a water-pot over the plants, will, in most cases, prevent the depredation of the black grub or cutworm.—Porcher, *Resources*, 107

HORSE-RADISH. Growing horse-radish is generally considered a matter of very little consequence, in regard to the matter of cultivation; and the result is, in most cases, small roots, which are inferior in flavor, are raised. It is very easy to grow this plant with roots as large as a man's wrist. Select a rich, warm piece of ground, fully exposed to the rays of the sun, and early in the

JOHN HAMMOND MOORE

season dig it deep. Mark it off for rows three feet apart, and haul the earth out of the rows, so as receive a heavy manuring, then cover the manure with the dirt taken from the rows and set the roots about eight inches apart. Keep free of weeds, as you would every other crop, and the result will be a growth of horse-radish that is worth growing.—*Field and Fireside*, January 2, 1864

HOPS. The hop vine makes a grateful arbor in summer. It grows luxuriantly in our climate. Its uses are various. It is a necessary element in all good yeast. It is a fundamental principle in the small beer and other malted liquors of the English, such as every English farmer knows how to manufacture, almost by nature. It may be bread and drink both, under proper management; and, if you raise barley also, who knows how much you will economize of life, how much secure of peace and enjoyment, in lessening the use of horrid whiskey? Somebody should begin the experiment, and why not you, or you, or you, whom we see with richly colored proboscis waiting at the corner for the slow coming of 12 o'clock?—*Tri-Weekly News*, April 20, 1865

ORDERS FROM MILLEDGEVILLE

Please watch the salt, wheat & corn and see they are not stolen. Salt is so high that the temptation is very great to steal it. Be sure to have the sow hunted up and kept in the clover lot until it is killed down and then have her put in the wheat field and she must be taken good care of when she has pigs. Have the cows taken care of and ask Mr. Land to purchase some shucks for me—say five large loads—and Bob must haul them. He can borrow Barstow's straw frame to haul with. See that the hogs are well fed, and warn Bob not to give them slop until it is cold.

**—Warren Akin to his wife in Cassville,
November 10, 1861, Akin Family Papers.**

Akin, later a Confederate congressman, then was a member of the state legislature.

137

PEANUTS. No one who raised peanuts last year will deny that they return more profit for less labor than any other crop that can be produced. Let there be plenty of them this year. They are good for the stock. Besides they make the best kind of oil—peanut oil being considered a much better oil than sperm; and, so long as there is such a demand for the article, peanuts will bring a high price. Let every planter have a large patch of peanuts. He will find it the most profitable crop he can raise.—*Southern Confederacy*, May 3, 1863

CROSSING COTTON WITH CORN! Mr. Kilpatrick, of this county, proposes to be one of ten planters in this neighborhood to cross their cotton with corn and turn over the proceeds to the families of absent soldiers. If he cannot find nine others, he will be one by himself to do it. Who will respond to this challenge to good works?

We find the above patriotic proposition in the *Telegraph* of Monday, says

---

I HAVE TO GIVE CORN FOR EVERY THING I BUY

You speak in your letter of selling corn to pay taxes, I do not think we will have any to spare, there is nothing to be had now except in exchange, I have to give Corn for Iron, Salt, Weaving, and indeed <u>every</u> thing that I buy, has to be paid in Provision, and the prospect of a crop now is very poor, we have no wheat to spare, and the corn here will not make but little, & I think we had best keep all we have, on hand until we see what we shall have, from this year; I do not still think it right to take high prices for Bread, and I see the Secretary of the Treasury advises for the People of South Carolina to do as the Noble Virginia Farmers have done (protest against high prices) but of course I am quite willing to submit to your judgment.

—Jane McLure of Union District, S.C., to her husband in Virginia, August 18, 1864, McLure Family Papers

---

JOHN HAMMOND MOORE

the *Macon Journal & Messenger*. We see it commended by several planters, to adopt the plan of crossing cotton rows with corn at intervals of twelve feet, with a furrow of corn, and plant at the intersection of every cotton row—thinning out to two stalks of corn. This diminishes the yield of cotton very slightly and will bring in a fair crop of corn.—*Southern Cultivator*, June 1861

BALE ROPE—A SUBSTITUTE. For roping cotton bales (says a correspondent of the *Macon Telegraph*), unravel some gunny-bagging, twist three strings of the warp into a cord, and then twist the cords into a rope, and you produce enough rope from one yard of bagging to rope a bale of cotton. Do not use raw hide, as it is liable to be destroyed by rats and vermin, and you will be charged $3 extra per bale when stored.—*Southern Cultivator*, March–April 1862

SALT FROM SMOKE HOUSES. Salt gotten from earth in smoke houses is better for all economical purposes than it looks. By running brine through pounded charcoal in a barrel its coloring matter will be separated. Boil it in clean kettles or pots, being careful to lift the salt, or skim it out, before the water is evaporated. In this way, all the salts of potash, soda, magnesia, and lime, which are more soluble than common salt, are left as bitters, with the sediment of gypsum, clay, and iron, in the bottom of the pot.—*Field and Fireside*, November 8, 1862

NIGHT SOIL—ITS VALUE. The best of all manures is the one which in our country is almost universally wasted. In Belgium, where agriculture is carried to great productiveness, they order things differently. There the estimate is by nice calculation that it is worth $10 for every man, woman, and child. We traverse sea and land, send to Africa and South America to bring elements of fertility which at home we throw away on every farm in the country. What an immense amount is wasted in our cities! It must be the most valuable, containing the elements of all kinds of food consumed by man, and in returning these to the soil, we return the identical constituents which former crops and animals have taken from the land. Night soil contains the phosphate of lime, which is indispensable to the growth of animal bones, and to the nutriment of plants, and which is not supplied from the atmosphere, like carbonic acid and ammonia. All fluid and solid excretions should be preserved by mixing them with burnt clay, saw dust, ashes, peat, or wood charcoal, &c. We have a great deal to learn, and alas! much more to practice that we have learned.—*Field and Fireside*, June 27, 1863

PLANTATION HYGIENE. Clean out thoroughly your negro quarters— scrape the yards and haul off to the turnip patches all of the refuse. Clean, scald, and whitewash the houses, *inside*, and sprinkle coal dust liberally about the premises.

FARM IMPLEMENTS. Are not improved by exposure to the sun, rain, &c.—get them all together—assort your hoes, repair tools, and put such under cover as may be injured by exposure. Put everything about the place in order, repair fences, stables, barns, clean out springs, open branches, and be ready for cotton picking, wheat sowing, and fall work.—*Farmer and Planter,* August 1861

SQUIRREL SKIN SHOES. Squirrel skins tacked down to a board, with hickory ashes sprinkled over them for a few days to facilitate the removal of the hair, and then placed in a strong decoction of red oak bark, will, at the end of four days make excellent leather, far stronger and tougher than calf-skin. Four skins will make a pair of lady's shoes.—*Edgefield Advertiser,* March 16, 1864

A SUBSTITUTE FOR SHOES. An old and experienced citizen has called to our attention, says the *Montgomery Advertiser & Register,* the subject of the use of cowhide moccasins as a substitute for shoes. He states when he moved to Mississippi, fifty-two years ago, no shoes were to be had for negroes, and they made their own out of this material, which answered the purpose as well as the elaborately made article, and in some respects better. The process is simple: Take green cowhide, or one well soaked, with hair on—which is to go next to the foot—"put the foot down firmly" upon it, cut out the pattern desired, make the necessary holes along the edges, and lace it up with a thong of the same material at the heel and up the instep. Let it dry upon the foot, and it accommodates itself perfectly to the shape of the latter, while it is sufficiently substantial for all kinds of traveling, and its elasticity is preserved by use. Socks should be put on when it is made, though it can be worn without . . . . The hair lining gives the advantage of warmth, so that socks, when not to be had, can be better dispensed with when moccasins are used than if shoes were worn. The gentleman to whom we are indebted for this suggestion says he has mentioned the subject to soldiers, who are very much pleased with it, and say there is no reason why soldiers should go barefoot while so many hides are thrown away in camps.—*Field and Fireside,* January 10, 1863

FIRE IN THE WOODS. As this is the season of wild and high winds—as there are many stragglers, deserters, and other "gipsies" prowling about and building fires in the woods, and as the negroes (and some white men) are exceedingly careless with "combustibles," we deem it our duty to give our readers a few words of caution.

First, then—clean up your fence-corners near woods or timbered land—leaving a bare space of ten to fifteen feet on each side of the rails.

Second—never allow your servants, or anyone else, to make a fire in your woods, on any pretext, unless they first clean off a space of thirty or forty square feet. If a high wind arises, it is dangerous, even then.

Third—do not let your negroes "tote" firebrands thro' your yard, or from their houses to the fields. Unless the weather is excessively cold, they can keep themselves warm by working, and their habit of hovering and crowding around a few burning "chunks" is a waste of time and entirely unnecessary.

Lastly—keep your yards free from light trash and litter—furnish your negroes with matches to keep in their cabins—have ladders and water always on hand—never put hot ashes in a wooden box or barrel, and see that all fires in the negro quarters and the "big house" are put out at a reasonable hour of the night. We shall have much to say against rail fences, generally, hereafter.— *Southern Banner*, March 15, 1865

LAND MEASURE. Every farmer should have a good measure—a light stiff pole, just sixteen and a half feet long, for measuring land. By a little practice, he can learn to step a rod in five steps, which will answer very well for ordinary farm work. Ascertain the number of rods in the width and length of a lot you want to measure, and multiply one by the other, and divide by 160, and you have the number of acres, as 160 square rods make a square acre. If you want to lay off a square acre, measure thirteen rods on each side, and you have the thing very near.—*Southern Cultivator*, July–August 1862

MORE ADVICE FROM PETERSBURG, OCTOBER 27, 1864

You must make them Careful of fire both about the house and in the fields. I am glad to hear that you were So fortunate as to have a part of your Shoes made before Mr. Brown Closed his Shop. you must be [as] Saving of leather as possible for we wont have any for another year. there is 2/3 of a hide at Finleys that if you have not got it must be ready. it is a good Sized hide & would make Several pair of Shoes. it is the hide of the old black Cow & will be upper leather. let me hear from you and what you are doing and how the negroes are doing. you must make them mind you and each one attend to their respective duties.

—Mackintosh, ed., *"Dear Martha,"* 154

TO MEASURE HAY STACKS. "More than twenty years since," says an old farmer, "I copied this following method for measuring hay from an old publication; and, having verified the general accuracy, I have bought and sold by it, and I believe it may be useful to many farmers where the means of weighing are not at hand. Multiply the length, breadth, and height into each other; and, if the hay is somewhat settled, ten solid yards make a ton. Clover will take from ten to twelve solid yards per ton."—*Field and Fireside*, January 25, 1863

A PLAN FOR MEASURING CORN. Having previously levelled the corn in the house, so that it will be of equal depth throughout, ascertain the length, depth, and breadth of the bulk; multiply these dimensions together, and their product by four. Then cut off one figure to the right of the product obtained by the last multiplication. This is so many bushels, and the decimal fraction of a bushel, of shelled corn. If the corn is on the ear, substitute eight for four, and cut off one figure as before.—*Confederate States Almanac*, 1865

WORTH KNOWING. If you wish to drive a cut nail into seasoned oak timber, and not have it break or bend, just have a small quantity of oil nearby, and dip the nail before driving, and it will never fail to go. In making carts, or ploughs, this is a great advantage, for they are generally mostly of oak wood. In straightening old nails before using them, let it be done on wood, and with easy blows. If done on iron, they will be sure to break.—*Southern Watchman*, May 4, 1864

HARD CEMENT. The following cement has been used with great success in covering terraces, lining basins, soldering stones, &c., and everywhere resists the infiltration of water. It is so hard that it scratches iron. It is formed of ninety-three parts of well burned brick and seven parts of litharge made plastic with linseed oil. The bricks and litharge are pulverized; the latter must be reduced to a very fine powder. They are mixed together and enough of the linseed added. It is then applied in the manner of plaster, the body that is to be covered being previously wet with a mop or sponge.—*Edgefield Advertiser*, March 12, 1862

CEMENT FOR STOPPING LEAKS. A composition of four pounds of rosin, one pint of linseed oil, and one ounce of red lead, applied with a brush, will stop leaks in roofs, water casks, &c.—*Southern Banner*, October 1, 1862

CHEAP PAINT. Gas-tar mixed with yellow ochre makes an excellent green paint, well adapted for preserving coarse woodwork and iron rails.

TO MAKE ELASTIC VARNISH FOR UMBRELLA AND HAT CASES. To a pint of turpentine in a flask, add one ounce of gum-elastic, cut in very small pieces. Put in the cork slightly and set in a warm place where the heat may not be equal to that of hot water till the gum-elastic is dissolved, which may be effected in four or five hours. Then strain the solution through a strong linen or cotton sheet and add one pint of boiled linseed oil.—*Field and Fireside,* January 28, 1863

STAINING WOOD

To stain wood red, take two ounces of Brazilwood and two ounces of potash, mix them with a quart of water and let the composition stand in a warm place for several days, stirring it occasionally. With the liquor made boiling hot, brush over the wood until the desired depth of color is obtained. Then, with another brush, brush over the wood, while wet, with a solution of alum, in the proportion of two ounces of alum to one quart of water. For a pink or rose red, use double the quantity of potash.

For a less bright red, dissolve an ounce of dragon's blood in a pint of spirits of wine and brush over the wood with the tincture till the stain appears to be as strong as is desired, but this a rather lacquering than staining.

For a pink or rose red, add to the above infusion of Brazilwood two additional ounces of pearlashes, and use as before directed, but it is not necessary in this case to brush the wood with alum water. By increasing the proportion of pearlashes, the red may be rendered even paler.

To stain wood green, dissolve verdigris in vinegar, or put crystals of verdigris in water, and brush over the wood with this hot solution.

To stain wood blue, dissolve copper in diluted nitric acid, and brush it while hot several times over the wood. Then make a solution of pearlashes, in the proportion of two ounces to a pint of water, and brush over the stain made with copper till the color is perfectly blue.

The green stain made above with verdigris may be changed to blue by the solution of pearlashes. The sulphate of indigo, which may usually be had ready prepared for the dyers, when diluted with water, makes a blue stain.

To stain wood black, brush the wood several times with a decoction of logwood, then several times with common ink.

To make a very fine black, brush over the wood with a solution of copper in nitric acid for blue, and then logwood till all of the greenness of the copper solution is gone.

To stain wood purple, take an ounce of logwood and two drachms of Brazilwood, boil them together in a quart of water over a moderate fire. When one-half of the fluid has evaporated, strain the decoction and brush it several times over the wood. After the wood is dry, brush it over with a solution of a drachm of pearlashes in a pint of water.

To stain wood yellow, infuse an ounce of tumeric in a pint of spirits of wine. Let the mixture stand for several days, closely covered, shaking it occasionally. Brush over the wood this infusion. A reddish yellow may be given to the color by the addition of a little gum tragacanth. Diluted nitric acid will produce a similar color.—*Field and Fireside*, February 21, 1863

A BEAUTIFUL AND LASTING WHITEWASH. Take a quarter of a peck of unslacked lime and pour in it a kettle of boiling water. While the lime is slacking, add a half a gallon of stale chamber-lye. When the lime is perfectly slacked, dilute it with water to the proper consistence, and add to this mixture one-quarter of an ounce of Prussian blue. This will give you a beautiful and lasting wash, that will neither peel off nor turn yellow. By increasing the quantity of blue, you may make either a pale or dark blue; and, by adding yellow or red ochre, you may impart either of these tints to suit your taste.

TO REMOVE PANES OF GLASS. Put soft soap on the putty for a few hours, and it becomes as soft as if just put on, though the putty has become hard as stone.—*Confederate States Almanac*, 1864

BOY, D'YE HEAR THIS!

Before you pay three cents for a jews-harp, see if you can't make just as pleasant a noise by whistling--for such, nature furnished the machinery. And before you pay seven dollars for a figured vest, young man, find out whether your lady love would not be just as glad to see you in a plain one that cost half the money. If she wouldn't, let her crack her own walnuts and buy her own clothes.

—Central Georgian, **February 2, 1862.**

Glossary

Absquatulate - to leave, decamp; also to squat or sit.

Ad libitum - at pleasure, as one wishes.

Alder - any of a genus of trees or shrubs of the birch family growing in moist ground; bark often used for dyeing and tanning.

Alum - potassium aluminum sulfate (potash alum) or ammonium aluminum sulfate (ammonia alum), both often called common alum; used as an emetic, astringent, and styptic.

Angelica - any of a large genus of herbs of the carrot family, especially a species whose roots and fruit provide angelica oil, used in liquors and perfumes.

Anodyne - soothing, a substance that eases pain.

Antimony - an element of metallic appearance, tin-white in color, hard and brittle; various compounds used in medicines and pigments.

Antiperiodics - used to prevent periodic attacks, such as intermittent fevers.

Aquafortis - strong water, nitric acid, especially as applied to a weak grade of commercial acid.

Arabic powder - made from gum arabic, exuded by certain species of the acacia tree; used as an emulsifier, an adhesive, and in inks and pharmaceuticals; also known as gum acacia.

Assafoetida/asafetida - the fetid gum resin of various oriental plants of the carrot family; used as an antispasmodic.

Balsam - an aromatic, resinous substance obtained from various plants and trees.

Batting - cotton or wool in sheets; used in quilts and similar materials.

Bene/benne - also known as sesame, an East Indian herb whose seeds yield sesame oil.

Bergamot - a pear-shaped orange whose rind yields an oil used in perfumes.

Birdlime - a sticky substance, usually made from holly bark; sometimes smeared on twigs to trap small birds.

Black jack - a common oak *(quercus marilandica)* with a black bark found in the eastern United States.

Blue pills - pills made of prepared mercury; used as a laxative.

Bluestone - blue vitriol.

Boneset - any of several herbs of the aster family, also known as thoroughwort and argueweed; leaves and flowers used as a diaphoretic and tonic.

Bonny-clabber - see clabber.

Bran - the broken coat of the seed of cereal grains, separated from the flour or meal by sifting or bolting.

Brawn - flesh of a boar or swine, especially when boiled or pickled.

Brazilwood - the heavy dye-wood of an East Indian redwood, also called sapanwood; or, a similar wood from various tropical American trees of the senna family.

Brimstone - sulphur.

Bromine - a caustic, normally deep-red liquid with a disagreeable odor; used in dyes, medicines, and as a disinfectant.

Bushel - dry measure, four pecks or thirty-two quarts.

Calcine - to make or become powdery by action of heat.

Calomel - mercurous chloride, much used in medicine as a purgative and to destroy intestinal worms.

Camomile - any of a genus of plants of the aster family, especially the common European species having a strong-scented foliage and flower heads that contain a bitter medicinal principle used as an antispasmodic and diaphoretic.

Camphor - a tough, gumlike compound obtained from the wood and bark of the evergreen camphor tree; used as a diaphoretic, stimulant, and sedative.

Cantharides - a preparation of dried beetles, especially blister beetles.

Capsicum - a large genus of tropical herbs and shrubs of the potato family; guinea pepper and chili are chief sources of cayenne pepper, but common, garden-variety green peppers are the best-known of the capsicums.

Chamber lye - urine.

China briar - a species of the genus *Smilax*, also known as bull briar, cat briar, horse briar, and bastard bamboo. Indians of the Southeast used the tops as greens and made a sort of bread out of the roots.

China tree - a handsome Asiatic tree *(Melia azedarach)* of the mahogany family, planted in the United States as a shade tree; also called Chinaberry, Pride of China, and Pride of India.

Chlorate of potassa - a highly volatile, white granular powder now used as a reagent in dyeing, tanning, and making ink.

Clabber - thick milk in the process of souring; also called bonny-clabber.

Clay pipe - highly plastic and fairly pure clay of a grayish-white color, often used in making pipes and thus sometimes called "pipe clay."

Colombo/calumba - the root of a plant indigenous to Mozambique; sometimes used in medicines as a mild tonic and for stomach disorders.

Copperas - copper water, crystallized ferrous sulphate, also called green vitriol; used in dyeing, tanning, and making ink.

Corrosive sublimate - mercury chloride, a violent poison as well as a powerful antiseptic and preservative.

Decoction - an extract prepared by boiling or steeping a substance or substances in hot water.

Diaphoretic - possessing power to increase perspiration.

Dock - one of a genus *(Rumex)* of plants of the buckwheat family, usually troublesome weeds with long taproots; roots of yellow dock were used as a stomach tonic and purgative.

Drachm/dram - one-eighth of a fluid ounce.

Dragon's blood - resinous substance, usually dark red, derived from various trees, especially the fruit of a Malaysian palm *(Calamus draco)*.

Dredger - a flour sifter.

Dyspepsia - difficult or deranged digestion; indigestion.

Elder - any of a genus of shrubs and trees of the honeysuckle family bearing flat clusters of small white and pink flowers and black and red berries.

Expectorate - to discharge, as phlegm, by coughing, hawking, and spitting.

Farina - a fine meal made from cereals; also starch derived from potatoes.

Filbert - a hazelnut.

Fip - fi' penny, a five-cent piece.

Fire - in corn, term used to indicate the crop has turned yellow prematurely.

Founder - laminitis, inflammation of a horse's hoof, causing the animal to become lame and stumble.

Foxglove - any plant of a genus of the figwort family; its leaves yield digitalis.

Fulling earth - fuller's earth, a clay-like substance used in mills to scour, cleanse, and thicken cloth.

Gall - to cause a sore by rubbing, such as one caused by too tight a harness on a horse.

Gapes - a disease of young fowl caused by nematode worms; symptoms are coughing and labored breathing, often with neck extended and beak open.

Gill - one-fourth of a pint, pronounced "jil."

Guaiacum - any of several tropical American trees that provide a resin used in medicines as a remedy for gout, rheumatism, and skin diseases; substance also called methylcatechol.

Gum arabic - a gum obtained from several species of the mimosa family *(genus Acacia)*.

Gum elastic - rubber, caoutchouc.

Gum myrrh - a yellowish brown to reddish brown aromatic gum resin with a bitter, slightly pungent taste; now used in the manufacture of dentifrices and perfumes and as a tonic.

Gum tragacanth - a substance derived from various Asiatic and East European herbs of the pea family; it swells in water and is used in the arts and pharmacy.

Gutta-percha - a whitish-to-brown substance resembling rubber but containing more resin and changing less on vulcanization; obtained from the latex of several Malaysian trees.

Hartshorn - aqua ammonia, carbonate of ammonia, smelling salts; also called spirits of hartshorn.

Heaves - a disease, chiefly of horses, marked by permanent distension of air

147

vesicles, heaving of the flanks, and a persistent cough.

Hoarhound/horehound - a bitter mint with hoary, downy leaves; extract used as a stomach tonic and remedy for coughs and colds.

Homeopathy - theory or system of medical practice holding that disease is cured by remedies that produce on a healthy person effects similar to the symptoms of the complaint of the patient; remedies usually given in minute doses.

Indian meal - ground Indian corn or maize.

Iodate - to impregnate with iodine.

Isinglass - a semi-transparent, whitish, very pure form of gelatin prepared from the air bladders of certain fish; used in jellies and glues.

Ivory black - a fine black pigment made by calcining ivory; used as a dentifrice and in paints.

Jerusalem artichoke - a perennial American sunflower; tuber of the plant often used as a vegetable.

Julep - not necessarily alcoholic by nature nor from Kentucky, a julep can be a refreshing drink flavored with aromatic herbs.

Kersey - coarse, ribbed woolen cloth, named for a village in Suffolk, England.

Lactugarium/lactucarium - the dried milk juice of a prickly lettuce (*Lactuca virosa*) resembling opium in physical properties and formerly used as a sedative.

Laudanum - formerly any of various preparations of opium; now a tincture of opium.

Lavender - a European mint with spikes of small purple flowers that produce an aromatic oil.

Leaven - any substance used to produce fermentation, as in dough or liquids, especially a portion of fermenting dough reserved for this use; also, specifically yeast.

Lees - the dregs, that which settles at the bottom of a cask.

Lemon-grass - a tropical, Old World grass with many blossoms that provide lemon-grass oil.

Ley/lye - originally a strong alkaline liquor (chiefly potassium carbonate) obtained by leaching wood ashes and much used in soap-making and washing; now, any strong alkaline solution.

Linsey/linsey-woolsey - coarse cloth made of linen and wool, also cotton and wool; named for the village of Linsey in Suffolk, England.

Litharge - a fused form of lead monoxide; loosely, lead monoxide in any form.

Lobelia - a genus of herbaceous plants, widely distributed and often cultivated for the beauty of their flowers; in pharmacy, refers to the leaves and tops of Indian tobacco or any emetic weed; used as an antispasmodic and expectorant.

Logwood - a hard, brownish heartwood of Central America and the West Indies; used in dyeing.

Lopper - to curdle or coagulate milk; the term "loppered" is common in Scotland and some parts of the United States.

Low mallow - a well-known wild plant *(Malva rotundifolia)* with hairy stems and leaves, often called common, field, or wild mallow; its fluids have long been used to ease external inflammations.

Mullein/mullen - a common weed found along roadways in North America, consisting of a tall spike with yellow flowers and velvety leaves; sometimes called flannel plant or beggar's blanket, it has long been used for medicinal purposes.

Mush - meal, especially Indian meal, boiled in water.

Neat - a bovine, such as a cow or ox.

Nitre/niter - potassium nitrate, saltpetre.

Nubbin - a small or imperfect ear of corn.

Ox-gall - the gall of an ox, used for cleaning purposes, also in painting (light chrome yellow) and in pharmaceuticals.

Papspoon - a child's spoon.

Paregoric - a medicine that mitigates pain, an anodyne; specifically, camphorated tincture of opium.

Paste - in cooking, doughs of various consistencies; often those containing a large proportion of fat for the crusts of pies, tarts, and other pastries.

Pearlash - a form of potassium carbonate obtained from crude potash.

Peck - dry measure, eight quarts; four pecks equal a bushel.

Peruvian bark - cinchona, a bitter bark from Andean trees of the madder family that contains quinine.

Petit grain, oil of - a fragrant, yellowish substance obtained from the leaves and twigs of the sour orange and similar trees; used chiefly in perfumes, soaps, and cosmetics.

Pip - a disease of fowls marked by a scale that forms on the tongue.

Poke root - a coarse, perennial herb with white flowers and purple berries that often are used for dyeing.

Potash - potassium carbonate, especially from wood ashes; purified potash is called pearlash.

Potassium oxide - burnt or calcined potash, soluble in water; used extensively as a reagent and in the manufacture of potassium salts.

Poultice - a soft composition, usually heated, spread on a cloth, and applied to a sore or inflamed part of the body.

Pride of India - see China tree.

Prussian blue - any of several complex iron compounds used in dyeing.

Prussic acid - hydrocyanic acid, a colorless and poisonous substance with a bitter, almond-like odor.

Pyroligneous acid - a reddish brown liquid containing chiefly acid and methanol, also called wood vinegar.

THE CONFEDERATE HOUSEWIFE

Quassia - a drug extracted from certain tropical trees; used as a bitter tonic and remedy for thread-worms in children, also as an insecticide and a substitute for hops in brewing.

Rack - a framework to hold hay and fodder for animals.

Rennet - the lining membrane of the fourth stomach of a calf; an extract from it often used to curdle milk, as in making cheese or junket.

Resin - any of a class of solid and semi-solid substances exuded by certain trees and plants, used in medicines and the making of varnishes and plastics.

Rhodium - a rare element found especially in platinum ores and separated as a hard, grayish metal insoluble in acids; sometimes used to electroplate microscopes and instrument parts to prevent corrosion.

Roche alum - an alum-like substance derived from alunite (also called alumstone); a whitish mineral salt used in dyeing, medicines, and fireproofing.

Rod - in linear measure, 5 1/2 yards or 16 1/2 feet; 30 1/4 square yards equal one square rod.

Rood - in square measure, one-fourth of an acre, or forty square rods.

Rosin - the hard resin, amber-colored to almost black, left after distilling the volative oil of turpentine; used in varnishes, soaps, on violin bows, and as a drier of oils.

Sago - starch prepared from the pith of an East Indian and Malaysian palm; used in puddings and for stiffening textiles.

Sal ammonia - ammonium chloride, a white salt used internally as an expectorant, stimulant, diuretic, and diaphoretic, and externally as a cooling and stimulating wash for contusions; also for filling batteries, soldering flux, and textile printing.

Sal soda - sodium bicarbonate; used in baking sodas and carbonated beverages, among other things.

Saleratus/sal aeratus - baking soda; either of two salts used as leavening agents—sodium bicarbonate or potassium bicarbonate.

Saltpetre/saltpeter - potassium nitrate, niter or nitre; as medicine, in small doses, diminishes body heat, lowers the pulse rate, and acts upon urine secretion; large doses can produce vomiting, purging, convulsions, even death.

Sandalwood - fragrant heartwood of a parasitic Indo-Malaysian tree.

Saponify - to convert to soap.

Sarsaparilla - the dried root of various tropical species *(Smilax)*, used as a mild tonic.

Scantlings - small pieces of lumber, also refers to the upright studs of a house.

Scrag - lean and inferior end of a neck of veal, mutton, or beef.

Scranings - scraps.

Scratches - a mange-like inflammation of a horse's fetlock, usually confined to hind legs and caused by wet, muddy, or filthy conditions.

Scruple - a minute amount; in apothecary weight, twenty grains; three scruples equal a dram.

JOHN HAMMOND MOORE

Sea-stock - sea-stores, provisions.

Senna - dried leaves of a certain species of the genus *Cassia*, used as a purgative.

Shab-racks - saddle cloths; those made of goat skins often were used by European light cavalry.

Shorts - a by-product of wheat milling that includes the germ, fine bran, and some flour.

Skippers - maggots that infest meat, also called salt-worms.

Slabbers - profuse salivation in animals, now called slobbering; long thought to be caused by red clover, but recent research indicates a fungus found in the clover, not the plant itself, is the culprit.

Snake root - any of a number of plants reputed to cure snake bites.

Sorghum - a tropical cereal grass cultivated as grain and forage or as a source of syrup.

Sorrel - any of a variety of plants with sour juice; also a plant of the genus *Rumex*, especially common sorrel and sheep sorrel, plants with acidic, pleasant-tasting leaves, found in dry places.

Spermaceti - a waxy solid obtained from oil of the sperm whale, used in making candles and cosmetics.

Spirits - a liquid produced by distillation, often called an extract or essence.

Squill - a bulbous herb of the lily family; bulbs and roots used as an expectorant, cardiac stimulant, and diuretic.

Staggers - a nervous disorder that causes an animal to reel and fall down; often called blind staggers.

Stirabout - a porridge of oatmeal or cornmeal boiled in water and milk and stirred.

Strangury - slow and painful discharge of urine.

Suet - hard fat around the kidneys of cattle and sheep; used in cooking and making tallow.

Sugar of lead - lead acetate, a colorless crystalline salt.

Sulphuric ether - a variant term for ether.

Suppuration - act or process of generating pus.

Sweeney - in horses, an atrophy of the muscles, especially in the shoulder.

Sweet oil - any mild edible oil, as olive oil.

Tag lock - a handful of twisted wool or hair.

Tansey/tansy - a member of the aster family, a plant with aromatic odor, bitter taste, and tonic principles.

Tartaric acid - an organic compound used in effervescent beverages, confections, and baking powders.

Thoroughwort - see boneset.

Tincture - a slight trace or vestige, often a solution of a medical substance in a mixture of alcohol.

Treacle - molasses, especially that drained from vats during the refining of sugar.

THE CONFEDERATE HOUSEWIFE

Tumeric/turmeric - an East Indian perennial herb of the ginger family; used as a coloring agent (yellow to reddish brown) and as a condiment with curry.

Turk's head - a round cake pan with a conical cone in the center.

Unslacked/unslaked - refers to lime or bulk coal that has not been crumbled or disintegrated.

Verdigris - a green or greenish-blue, poisonous pigment and drug obtained by action of acetic acid on copper.

Vitriol - a sulfate of various metals in crystallized form, especially copper (blue vitriol).

Whey - the watery part of milk that separates from the thick or coagulated part (curd) when making cheese.

Whiting - chalk (calcium carbonate) prepared as a powder by pulverizing and washing.

Whortleberry - a European blueberry, sometimes called huckleberry.

Wormwood - a European woody herb, especially one species yielding a bitter, slightly aromatic dark green oil used in making absinthe.

Yeast powder - baking powder, a mixture of soda or saleratus with cream of tartar (tartaric acid).

JOHN HAMMOND MOORE

Sources

Georgia Newspapers and Periodicals
Albany Patriot
Central Georgian (Sandersville)
Clarke's Confederate Household Almanac (Vicksburg and Macon)
Confederate States Almanac (Macon)
Gate City Guardian (Atlanta)
Rome Tri-Weekly Courier
Southern Banner (Athens)
Southern Confederacy (Atlanta)
Southern Cultivator (Augusta and Athens)
Southern Enterprise (Thomasville)
Southern Federal Union (Milledgeville)
Southern Field and Fireside (Augusta)
Southern Literary Gazette (Athens)
Southern Recorder (Milledgeville)
Southern Watchman (Athens)

South Carolina Newspapers and Periodicals
Abbeville Banner
Camden Confederate
Camden Daily Journal
Carolina Spartan (Spartanburg)
Charleston Daily Courier
Charleston Mercury
Charleston Tri-Weekly Courier
Charleston Tri-Weekly Mercury
Confederate Baptist (Columbia)
Daily South Carolinian (Columbia)
Due-West Telescope
Edgefield Advertiser
Farmer and Planter (Pendleton and Columbia)
Keowee Courier (Walhalla)
Laurensville Herald
Miller's Planters' and Merchants' Almanac (Charleston)
South Carolina Baptist (Columbia)

Southern Agriculturalist (Charleston and Laurensville)
Southern Almanac (Greenville)
Southern Christian Advocate (Charleston)
Southern Lutheran (Columbia)
Spartanburg Express
Tri-Weekly News (Winnsboro)
Tri-Weekly Watchman (Sumter)
Yorkville Enquirer

Books and Articles

Andrews, Eliza Frances. *The War-Time Journal of a Georgia Girl, 1864–1865.* New York, 1908.

Burge, Dolly Sumner Lunt. *A Woman's Wartime Journal.* New York, 1918.

Burroughs, Frances M. "The Confederate Receipt Book: A Study of Food Substitution in the American Civil War." *South Carolina Historical Magazine* (January 1992): 31–50.

Chance, Joseph E., ed. *The Mexican War Journal of Captain Franklin Smith.* Jackson, 1991.

The Confederate Receipt Book: A Compilation of Over One Hundred Receipts Adapted to the Times. Athens, 1960. Originally published in 1863.

Coxe, John Redman. *The American Dispensary. . . .*Philadelphia, 1827.

Dixie Cook-Book. Atlanta, 1882.

Dull, Mrs. S. R. *Southern Cooking.* Atlanta, 1928.

Edgeworth, Mary L., ed. *Southern Gardener and Receipt-Book.* Philadelphia, 1860.

Foster, Nelson, and Linda S. Cordell, eds. *Chilies to Chocolate: Food the Americas Gave the World.* Tucson and London, 1992. See especially "The Peripatetic Chili Pepper: Diffusion of the Domesticated Capiscums Since Columbus" by Jean Andrews, 81–93.

Gerstacher, Friedrich. *Wild Sports of the Far West.* London, 1854.

"Good Eatings." *Southern Literary Messenger* (May 1863): 304–11.

Goosequill, Abraham. "My Uncle Simon's Plantation." *Southern Literary Gazette* (October 21, 1848): 186–87.

Hess, Karen. *The Carolina Rice Kitchen: The African Connection.* Columbia, 1992.

Hess, Karen, ed. *Martha Washington's Booke of Cookery.* New York, 1981.

Hess, Karen, ed. *The Virginia House-Wife.* Columbia, 1984. Originally published in 1824.

Hill, Mrs. A. P. *Housekeeping Made Easy.* New York, 1867.

Hollingsworth, C. Dixon, Jr. "The Story of Barbecue." *Georgia Historical Quarterly* (Fall 1979): 391–95.

Jones, Evan. *American Food: The Gastronomic Story.* New York, 1975.

Kollock, Susan M., ed. "Letters of the Kollock and Allied Families, 1826–1884." *Georgia Historical Quarterly.* Published in five parts, December 1949–March 1951.

Leland, Isabella Middleton, ed. "The Middleton Correspondence, 1861–1865." *South Carolina Historical Magazine.* Published in ten parts, January 1962–April 1964.

Lerner, William, chief director. *Historical Statistics of the United States: Colonial Times to 1970.* 2 vols. Washington, 1975.

Livingston-Little, D. E., ed. *The Mexican War Diary of Thomas D. Tennery.* Norman, Okla., 1970.

Logone, Jan. "Portable Soup." *Journal of Gastronomy* 1, no. 4 (1985): 52–59.

Mackintosh, Robert Hurley, Jr., ed. *"Dear Martha . . .," The Confederate War Letters of a South Carolina Soldier, Alexander Faulkner Fewell.* Columbia, 1976.

Massey, Mary Elizabeth. *Ersatz in the Confederacy.* Columbia, 1952.

Porcher, Francis Peyre. *Resources of the Southern Fields and Forests. . . .* Charleston and Richmond, 1863.

Richardson, Emma B., ed. "The Letters of William Richardson, 1765–1784." *South Carolina Historical Magazine* (January 1946): 1–20.

Robertson, Ben. *Red Hills and Cotton.* New York, 1942.

Ross, Fitzgerald. "A Visit to the Cities and Towns of the Confederate States, 1864–1865." *Blackwood's Edinburgh Magazine* (February 1865): 151–75. Later published in book form by Blackwood's.

Roth, Darlene, ed. *The Atlanta Exposition Cookbook.* Athens, 1984. Originally published as *Tested Recipe Cook Book* in 1895.

Rozier, John, ed. *The Granite Farm Letters.* Athens and London, 1988.

Rutledge, Anna Wells, ed. *The Carolina Housewife.* Columbia, 1979. Originally published in 1847.

Scott, Edwin J. *Random Recollections of a Long Life.* Columbia, 1884.

Spartanburg Dames' Recipe Book. Spartanburg, 1902.

Tennent, Mrs. E. R., ed. *House-Keeping in the Sunny South.* Atlanta, 1885.

Thornton, Phineas. *The Southern Gardener and Receipt Book.* Newark, 1845. Originally published in 1840.

Walker, Ralph, trans. "An Arkansas Barbecue." *Early American Life* (August 1984): 30–31, 75.

Williams, J. F. *Old and New Columbia.* Columbia, 1929.

Unpublished Materials

South Carolina Historical Society, Charleston, South Carolina, Vanderhorst Papers.

South Caroliniana Library, University of South Carolina, Columbia, South Carolina, Diaries and papers of the Alston Family, Mary Boykin Chesnut, Emma Holmes, James Kershaw, Mackenzie Family, Alexander McLeod Family, and John William McLure Family.

Special Collections, University of Georgia Library, Athens, Georgia, Jennie Akehurst Diary and Akin Family Papers.

Winthrop University Archives, Rock Hill, South Carolina, David Golightly Harris Journals.

JOHN HAMMOND MOORE

Index

THE CONFEDERATE HOUSEWIFE